Cancer Chronicles

One man's journey to glorify God through illness

Bill Williams
Edited by Melissa Wren Brown
Foreword by Dr. Tim Presson

Copyright © 2011 Bill Williams
All rights reserved.

ISBN: 146373834X
ISBN 13: 9781463738341

Library of Congress Control Number: 2011916122
CreateSpace Independent Publishing Platform
North Charleston, South Carolina

In honor of Clyde "Bill" Williams Jr.
August 30, 1950 – August 17, 2007

This book is a collection of praises to a magnificent God for His mercies, love, and grace during trials. God showed his servant, Bill, how to enjoy and glorify Him, regardless -of the circumstances. Bill realized that this life was never about him; it was about His Savior, Jesus Christ.

"It does not belong to us, Lord. The glory belongs to you because of your love and loyalty."

PSALM *115:1*

"For to me, to live is Christ, and to die is gain."

PHILIPPIANS *1:21*

Contents

ACKNOWLEDGEMENTS	VII
FOREWORD:	
Dr. Tim Presson	*ix*
PROLOGUE:	
Prayers Foreshadowing Illness	*xiii*
INTRO:	
Bill's Journal Entry: I've Got Cancer	*xvii*
LETTER 1:	
Counting our Blessings	*1*
LETTER 2:	
When God Answers Prayers His Way	*5*
LETTER 3:	
Mans' Medical Options	*15*
LETTER 4:	
Second Opinion at Mayo Clinic	*21*
LETTER 5:	
Accepting Our Daily Bread	*29*
LETTER 6:	
The Lord is my Shepherd	*39*
LETTER 7:	
Stem Cell Transplant	*47*
LETTER 8:	
Life after Stem Cell	*57*
LETTER 9:	
The Cancer Returns	*65*

LETTER 10:
   Contentment in God's Will   71
LETTER 11:
   Near Death with Spinal Meningitis   77
LETTER 12:
   A State of Thankfulness   85
LETTER 13:
   "What Condition My Condition Is In"   91
LETTER 14:
   Testing the Genuineness of our Faith   97
LETTER 15:
   In Christ Alone   101
PROMISES:
   The Rainbows God Sent   107
DEATH:
   The "Good Fight" is Over   109
WIFE'S LETTER:
   Jan Williams   111
DAUGHTER'S LETTER:
   Melissa Wren Brown   115
SCRIPTURE REFERENCES
BIOGRAPHY:
   Bill Williams   127
CONTACT INFO:
   Grace Community Church   129
   StoneWater Church   129
RESOURCES:
   Multiple Myeloma Cancer   131
SUGGESTED READING   132

Acknowledgments

Our family would like to thank the friends at Grace Community Church in Glen Rose, Texas, who have supported and loved us over the last thirteen years.

Thank you to Tim and Lynn Presson and Brent and Kristi Thomas for ministering, encouraging us, and being such a big part of our lives.

To Ike and Trisha Thomas and family, who have been a part of our family for over 36 years. Words cannot express our gratitude for all you've done. We love you!

To Maurice and Carol Walton, who if it hadn't been for you inviting Bill to your Bible study when he was 36, all of our lives might be different. Thank you for being special friends.

To the friends at StoneWater Church in Granbury, Texas, who uplifted our family with warm embraces during this time. Thank you for planting, what Marley and Tessa, Bill's granddaughters, refer to as the "Popa Tree," in their front yard. It is forever a reminder of your love.

To our neighbors in Bluffview Estates and the "Padre Pals" who were constantly there to meet our needs before we even knew they needed to be met. Multiple thanks and praise God!

The good Lord has blessed us with amazing friendships throughout the community of Granbury, Texas, as well as miraculous experiences with people from all over the world. We are blessed beyond measure.

Foreword:
by Dr. Tim Presson

Perhaps once in your lifetime, you might hope to be privileged by the Lord's sweet providence in bringing one of his special servants into your life. My life was eternally blessed to have had that special mercy of God expressed in my life in 1999. That's when I first met Bill Williams, a man that the Lord would use extraordinarily in my life both in his living and his dying. From sweating profusely on mission trips to China to snow ball fights at conferences in Minnesota, Bill became a living display of what the humble Christian life ought to be.

I'll never forget that day. It was on August, 17, 2007, my oldest son's 18th birthday. The Lord had taken one of my best friends home at precisely the time that my eldest had been born those 18 years before. I consider it to be such sweet providence.

As I consider Bill's life, it moves me to think about the enormous impact he had on the lives of so many people. Certainly Bill would have been the last person to agree with such a statement. I believe it to be precisely for that reason that his life impacted so many! Without exception, every time I went to visit Bill during his health battle (whether in a hospital or at home) with the intention of encouraging him, I walked away with the very clear realization that just the opposite had occurred. Invariably, I walked away challenged, refreshed, encouraged and desiring to live my life more to the glory of God. If I've ever been privileged to live life alongside someone who desired to redeem every moment to the glory of God more than Bill, I certainly don't know who it would be. My life has been eternally enriched by the opportunity to have served alongside one of God's choice servants.

In a day in which it's rare to truly find a "churchman," Bill stood out as one who had a legitimate burden, yearning, desire, and jealousy for the purity of Christ's body, the Church. Cancer never became the placard over Bill's life. He refused to permit his illness to become the clarion call that defined his life, his identity, his persona. He actively resisted allowing it to become his consuming conversation piece. Instead, he sought the Lord and was allowed by the Lord to see his sickness redirect attention away from himself to the One whom he relentlessly regarded as supreme in all of life. Bill has helped teach me not only how to live well, but also how to die well. That is indeed an uncommon laboratory of experience in this world.

I certainly grieve the loss of all that the Lord used Bill to bring to my life and that of his family and friends, but am also able to affirm with great joy the truth of what Paul said to the Thessalonian believers: "We do not grieve as others who have no hope" (1 Thess. 4:13). Indeed, hope was a hallmark produced by the Holy Spirit of God in Bill's life. It wasn't the hope that this world seeks to offer – it was that glorious and blessed hope that has God as its foundation.

The night he passed, I sat down after having received the call about Bill's death and reflected on his life. Those reflections became the basis of the following poem:

Foreword: by Dr. Tim Presson

"The Beatific Vision Now Realized"

The memories forever etched;
the impact endlessly sketched.
The life lived now beholding
the One who is continuously unfolding
His brilliance and glory before the eyes
of his child now seeing that which defies
the explanation or words of this finite life
now walking in glorious sight without strife.

A dear friend gone home to our mutual rest;
a fellow servant now infinitely blessed
with the reward of a life lived for the goal
of reaching the prize of his redeemed soul.
The beatific vision of his Savior now real,
which no thief can ever break in and steal.
We grieve our losses in this earthly tent,
yet know the reason for which He was sent –
To glorify His Father and make us one
by the perfect sacrifice by which we were won.

Sickness is now no more a distress
concerning which my brother has need to address.
He is now whole and in perfect delight
in the One by whom he fought the good fight.
Laid up for him is that beautiful treasure
of the One who alone was his definitive pleasure.
Therefore, our grief is but for a moment in time
until we, too, behold the eternally sublime.
May the lessons be learned, the significance felt,
until every hindrance and obstruction does finally melt
into that ultimate joy beyond this sod
as fellow worshipers of the one living God!

May the reflections of this book be used of the Lord as Bill's life was used: to glorify God and enjoy Him forever!

Dr. Tim Presson
Fort Worth, Texas

Prologue:

Prayers Foreshadowing Illness

March 10, 2002: Bill's journal entry

My days are numbered upon this earth, and no one will remember them but for a short season. I thank you God for those given to me. You could have easily taken me at age nine, during my almost-fatal battle with spinal meningitis, but you chose to leave me for your own purpose. Help me to recognize that purpose and honor you with my life. (References to Psalm 6:5: "No one remembers you when he is dead. Who praises you from the grave?")

March 12, 2002: Bill's journal entry

Thank you Father for Your protection of me. I know that I will not live one day longer than that which you have ordained for me, and you may choose to remove me in a tragic manner, yet I am comfortable now and rest in Your sovereign will. Who am I to complain when You do all things for the good of those who love you? (Reference to Romans 8:28 and Psalm 7:1-2: "O Lord my God, I take refuge in you; save and deliver me from all who pursue me, or they will tear me like a lion and rip me to pieces with no one to rescue me.")

January 1, 2005: Bill's journal entry

For the last year I've consistently prayed for the following in my life:

1. That I would not perish in a rest home where I might so dishonor my Lord with ill behavior.

2. That I would be taught to number my days so they might be used more productively in His service and not my own.

3. That I need to be less involved in business affairs and more focused on His work, and I don't know how to correct my course. Give me direction.

Prologue:

POINTS TO PONDER

- The purpose of humanity is to glorify God and enjoy Him forever. See 1 Corinthians 10:31 and Psalm 16:11. Is your life reflecting such purpose?

  _____

  _____

- Ask the Lord to help you properly number your days, so that you might be more productive in His service. See Psalm 90:12.

  _____

  _____

- Before you can adequately prepared to live, you must be adequately prepared to die. Matthew 16:26 – "For what will it profit a man if he gains the whole world and forfeits? Or what shall a man give in return for his soul?"

  _____

  _____

Introduction:

Bill's Journal Entry – I've Got Cancer

December 16, 2004

It's now been three weeks to the day that my Heavenly Father reached down and entangled my weakened step with a gas hose in Round Rock, Texas. Little did I realize that the ensuing fall and breaking of my left arm would prove to be a merciful act by God.

My family and I had just spent a wonderful Thanksgiving Day at the home of my younger daughter Kendra, our son-in-law Kevin, his parents, Fran and Jean, and our two-year-old granddaughter, Marley. Melissa, my older daughter, and Jan, my wonderfully patient wife, and I departed from Austin around six that evening with intentions of returning to Granbury. We needed to make one stop for gasoline, and we would be on our way.

The next thing I remember is the surreal feeling of being in slow motion, tripping over the gas hose connected to my car. I felt my left arm snap but thought it had dislocated my shoulder because the fall was not severe enough to have broken the upper bone of my arm. Jan helped me up and put me in the driver's side of her Jeep Cherokee before helping me into the passenger seat. My arm dangled at my side, useless.

The pain was more than my body could tolerate, and I immediately became soaked in a cold sweat. I was nauseous, could not focus mentally on what I should do next. Thankfully, Jan quickly contacted Kendra on where we might find the closest hospital and found one within fifteen minutes. Oh, how I was relieved to be in the Georgetown ER. However, it being a holiday, it was packed and became evident that they only had the minimum number of employees staffing the facility.

We spent four hours there and left with a partial cast and an x-ray showing that I had a broken arm, not a dislocated shoulder. The doctor on duty strongly cautioned me to make an appointment with a specialist as soon as possible because he said this break shouldn't have occurred. He considered it to be a pathologic or secondary reason for the break.

We spent the night in Round Rock and left for Granbury Friday morning. We were able to meet with our local doctor at his clinic around noon, and we left the x-rays for him to review. Saturday and Sunday were a blur to me because I remained on pain killers throughout the weekend. My doctor asked if I would come by Monday for standard blood work which we completed by noon Monday.

At around 4:00 p.m. the phone rang, and Jan answered it. It was my doctor's office calling to report on my blood work. I rested while Jan visited. I must have napped momentarily because the next thing I recall is Jan kneeling by my chair in our living room and telling me we were headed to Baylor All Saints in Ft. Worth, where a room had been prepared for me and a doctor from the oncology department would be assisting us.

Introduction:

I could tell Jan was visibly shaken, and her emotions were seeping out, as she attempted to remain strong with this news. My outward emotions were stoic, but inwardly I was sickened, scared and felt that I wasn't actually experiencing this tale of horror. Reality was more than I could handle at the moment.

Suddenly my left arm took on a totally different dimension as my thoughts turned to the unthinkable. I've got cancer.

Points To Ponder

*"God would prefer we have an occasional limp than a perpetual strut.
And if it takes a thorn for him to make his point,
He loves us enough not to pluck it out."*

MAX LUCADO

- The late Oxford English Literature scholar, C. S. Lewis, spoke of certain acts of God that might appear to us as awful, yet ought to be considered by us as "severe mercies." In what ways can you see unpleasant events in your life as actually being acts of God's severe mercy?

_____

_____

- What are some things that we can actively do in order not to take God's blessings in our lives for granted?

_____

_____

- We will undoubtedly face times of great fear in this life, but we find encouragement in the Scriptures:

Introduction:

> Psalm 27:1 – "The Lord is my light and my salvation; whom shall I fear? The Lord is the stronghold of my life; of whom shall I be afraid?"

> 1 Peter 5:7 instructs us to cast all our anxieties on him, because we know that he cares for us.

> Hebrews 2:14-15 says, "Since therefore the children share in flesh and blood, he himself likewise partook of the same things, that through death he might destroy the one who has the power of death, that is, the devil, and deliver all those who through fear of death were subject to lifelong slavery."

_____

_____

- How many times have you asked yourself, "Why God? Why me? Why is this happening?" What does Paul say in Romans 9:20-21? "But who are you, O man, to talk back to God? Shall what is formed say to him who formed it, 'Why did you make me like this?' Does not the potter have the right to make out of the same lump of clay some pottery for noble purposes and some for common use?"

_____

_____

- God is the potter; we are His clay. It is not for us to ask "Why?", but rather ask "How will You use this, Lord?"

  _____

  _____

LETTER 1:

Counting our Blessings

December 16, 2004

Dear family and friends,

Today marks three weeks since Bill fell. We consider it a blessing that he broke his arm because we now know that he has Multiple Myeloma, "a cancer of the plasma cells, a type of white blood cells present in the bone marrow," according to the Mayo Clinic.

As most of you know, Bill tripped over a hose at a gas station in Georgetown. After a visit to the emergency room, our lives have taken a route we weren't expecting. He was admitted to Baylor All Saints in Fort Worth on November 29, 2004, and stayed until December 2nd. He was poked, prodded, punched and pampered.

Now we're home recuperating and trying to be patient. Melissa was his nurse last week while I worked, and I'm his nurse this week. Bill's been a great patient, considering he's never been one to sit around or to take medication.

At this point, we're just trying to take it one day at a time. He's been able to work a little from the house, and Melissa has done quite a lot of correspondence. Brenda, his business manager, has also been a great help taking charge at the office. Bill cannot drive due to the broken arm, so he only gets to go to the office when one of us takes him.

We go back to the oncologist on December 21st and have an appointment with the stem cell doctor in Dallas on January 3rd. We all feel we might know more by then and will be able to get our plan of action into high gear.

Bill and I love the Lord dearly. We know He is a sovereign God whose plan for each of us is perfect. He makes no mistakes, and He designs all circumstances for our good. Our hope and strength rests with Him.

Christmas is a special time to celebrate the birth of our Lord. We'll be spending it with our daughters, son-in-law and granddaughter at home. May this holiday season be a time to count your blessings. We are counting ours.

Love, Jan

Points To Ponder

"Faith is not the belief that God will do what you want. Faith is the belief that God will do what is right."

MAX LUCADO

- God redeems our suffering without eliminating it.

　　_____

　　_____

- Do you believe God's plan for you is perfect, even if He answers your prayers by giving you something other than what you asked for, like cancer... or if He gave it to you in a different way than you expected it to be answered?

　　_____

　　_____

- Jeremiah 29:11: "For I know the plans I have for you," declares the Lord, "plans to prosper you and not to harm you, plans to give you hope and a future."

　　_____

　　_____

- Do you want God's will for your life more than your own will, even if it means getting a disease or another illness? What do you fear most?

  _____

  _____

- How much of the focus of your life is spent on distancing yourself from pain and discomfort instead of receiving it as a means of making you more like your Savior?

  _____

  _____

- Romans 8:28: "And we know that in all things God works for the good of those who love him, who have been called according to his purpose."

  _____

  _____

"Resolved, never to do anything which I should be afraid to do if it were the last hour of my life."

JONATHAN EDWARDS

LETTER 2:

When God Answers Prayers His Way

January 1, 2005

Dear family and friends,

It's New Year's Day evening, and on behalf of our family to yours we hope your holiday was as bountiful and blessed as ours. When you consider that most in this world lack the basics in life and have still never heard what the "Christ" in Christmas means, you must confess that we in this country have been blessed by a merciful God. We sincerely thank you for the calls, meals, cards and visits. They always cheer our hearts, and we are most grateful for the many prayers – we do feel them!

Just a brief update as to what is occurring with my treatments and my present condition. We visited my oncologist on December 21st, and the blood work reflected that the blood count was good and above the level of needing additional transfusions. This was great news in that I had received four pints of blood approximately five weeks ago while in the hospital and the transfused blood has begun to dissipate. I received a Procrit shot upon leaving the hospital, and it's apparently assisted my system in generating new blood.

Dr. Mary Milam, my oncologist, asked that I return to her office in one month for an additional check-up. It will be this next visit that we should find out whether or not the oral chemo program I'm currently on is fighting the Multiple Myeloma in my system. I'm taking Thalidomide daily and rotating steroids every four days. Should this combination work without too many serious side effects, then I'll be on it indefinitely at this point.

Next Steps: Life Changes

Our next trip to visit a doctor will be January 3rd when we will visit the office of Dr. Robert Collins, located at UT Southwestern in Dallas. He will be my stem cell transplant doctor. We'll learn more about the procedure and what type of stem cell transplant will be utilized.

We're uncertain at this point as to whether they will harvest my own, where they have developed methods of removing cancerous tumors from the stem cells or whether they'll request that I seek a donor. Should donors be sought then packets will first be sent to my siblings in that they are my more probable possibility of matching.

My most difficult journey will be surviving the heavy chemo treatment just prior to the stem cell transplant. Heavy chemo is given to destroy all existing cancer in my system with hopes of not destroying key organs in the process. Unfortunately, each of us differ in how our bodies tolerate poison, and recovery from the chemo may vary from months or the rest of my lifespan. I will covet your prayers most during this period, which we anticipate could be February or March. I'll be in isolation for up to four to six weeks in Dallas while my immune system builds back.

Concerning my daily life, it's changed rather dramatically. I can dress myself, but bathing and grooming is another issue. My broken arm is only in a sling, without a cast, so I am most cautious with my movements. I feel like a bowl of rice crispies when I move or bend the wrong way and feel and hear the snap, crackle, pop sounds. I must confess that it appears the humerus bone is becoming more secure, and I have hopes that it will be just a few more months of healing.

The problem with this arm healing is the break occurred where the cancer manifested itself most. Thus, the cancer medicine must first stop its destruction, so my body can heal itself. My orthopedic surgeon said it may take up to one year before the arm will be fully functional. I hope she's wrong. We visit her on January 19th for new x-rays on the arm.

As to my physical state, I've been shocked as to how much I've weakened over the past four weeks. Perhaps it's partly mental, but the reality truly surprised me. The days I'm on steroids I feel about seventy-five percent normal with the exception of having very low stamina. It's on these days that I attempt to take care of business issues and make the most of my days.

However, for the four days I'm without the artificial energy from the steroids my system begins to come to a halt. My oncologist said I'd feel like garbage on these days, and she was right. Each of these days get increasingly worse, wherein the last day has proven to be my "flu day," in that's how I feel. All of my joints ache, and all my energy seems to have left town. I've found it hard to focus on much on these days.

My Relationship with Christ

As to my spiritual state of mind, I can say that I've never been closer to my Lord and Savior than what I've experienced over these past four weeks. Yet I had one particular day that I struggled mightily all day with every one of my beliefs. Never have I seen a deeper black hole or a more fiery-hell than what my mind experienced that day.

It was truly a test for me, and had it not been for my Savior's loving hands pulling me away from the pit and His caring and devoted arms to embrace my deeply troubled, doubting soul, I shiver to think of the bitterness of soul I might have emerged with. I cannot fathom anyone experiencing that kind of darkened day without the strength of Christ.

Thankfully my dark day has passed, and I've experienced no others. I praise my God – the triune God Head, Father, Son and Holy Ghost daily and rest in His strength and guidance in my life.

For the last year I've prayed consistently for the following in my life: 1) That I would not perish in a rest home where I might so dishonor my Lord with ill behavior. 2) That I'd be taught to number my days so they might be used more productively in His service and not my own. 3) That I need to be less involved in business affairs and more focused on His work, but I don't know how to correct my course. Give me direction.

I can safely say that God has responded to my prayers, answering them all with one small fall. It was not the answer I was expecting, but then again God says, "For my thoughts are not your thoughts, neither are your ways my ways." (Isaiah 55:8) So, it is *me* who must adjust to His answer.

What Every Christian Should Expect

My family and I believe in and worship a very sovereign God. One who brings hardships, illness, and even death to his beloved in order to test, strengthen, punish and sanctify us in preparation for spending eternity in His kingdom. Those that are His children can all expect some, if not all of the above to occur in your life as well. Perhaps it will not be a battle with cancer. It might be a divorce, loss of a job, or the loss of a child. However, rest assured that every child of His will be tested, punished and "pruned" so that you will be more fruitful, giving Him more honor.

So, I caution you to plant your spiritual roots deeply, where the spring of "living water" flows because new storms are headed your way to test that root system. "He will not let you be tempted beyond what you can bear" (1 Corinthians 10:13). But, you will exceed what you consider bearable because He will place you in a position of full dependence upon Him, as He did with the Israelites when He led them for forty years in an inhospitable environment in the desert, where no human could survive for a few days, much less years, without His loving and nurturing care.

It's this same dependence I find myself in, and it's truly been frightening at times, but mostly it's been comforting, peaceful and hopeful. If I should not survive the year, I know His work for me is complete, and my days on this earth will have ended as planned. "Man's days are determined; you have decreed the number of his months and have set limits he cannot exceed" (Job 14:5).

Should He choose to leave me here, then I know my remaining days will be spent differently in that each will truly be numbered, and my business affairs will be pushed as far back as possible as His work is placed as priority. I memorized a verse in the late eighties after He replaced my stony heart with a heart of flesh, which says, "I have been crucified with Christ, and I no longer live, but Christ lives in me. The life I live in the body, I live by faith in the Son of God, who loved me and gave himself for me" (Galatians 2:20).

This verse has always remained one of my favorites to review, but I had failed to fully understand its full implications - to comprehend what it means to be crucified with Christ, and that I no longer live. From the day he changed my heart, I've desired to serve Him and be led by Him, but I have done so under my terms and not His.

If I was crucified with Him, dying to how I once lived and wishing to follow new ways where I find myself now cleansed and justified in front of a Holy God that has accepted the blood of an innocent man as atonement for my many sins, then I must cease from anything pertaining to my desires and my terms. Nothing in my current life is on my terms; it is now all on His.

I've never fully comprehended what "I no longer live" means until now. I fully recognize, given the seriousness of this disease that I have in essence died and no longer live. What limited time I have must be spent in His service and not my own. I was bought with a price, the death of His son. How can I remain in pursuit of my own selfish ways?

God can choose to remove this illness by placing it in remission or leave it active, causing an agonizing death. Whatever He chooses, I wish only to be in His will and to honor Him with the remaining time allotted to me. I now realize, "I no longer live."

Our family is looking forward to 2005 because it will be another year of walking and trusting in our Lord. He's blessed us in so many ways, and we know that the trials sent our way are designed for our sanctification and ultimately for our good. We're thankful to worship such a God who loves us enough that He will "prune" us so we may produce more fruit, resulting in more honor and glory to Him, the Most High God.

It is in His peaceful, holy hands we rest and find our hope.

With love from all of us, Bill

Points To Ponder

*"Paul said, 'I die every day!'" 1 Corinthians 15:31.
John Piper said, "Daily Christian living is
daily Christian dying."*

- Do you have a relationship with Jesus Christ, and if so, what is it like? What is the basis of your relationship with Christ?

  _____

  _____

- The issue is not primarily one of how much faith you have, but rather one of the proper object of faith, which is Jesus Christ.

  _____

  _____

- "For it has been granted to you that for the sake of Christ you should not only believe in him but also suffer for his sake" Philippians 1:29.

  _____

  _____

- Spend some time reflecting on the fact that not only is belief in Christ a gift from God, but suffering is also.

  _____

  _____

- Paul said, "I am hard pressed between the two. My desire is to depart and be with Christ, for that is far better. But to remain in the flesh is more necessary on your account" Philippians 1:23-24.

  _____

  _____

- It is understandable that we would want to remain living for the sake of those we love, but is your longing to be with Christ in heaven greater than any love you have in this world?

  _____

  _____

- If you're ill, you're not alone unless you don't know Christ.

  _____

  _____

- If you died today, are you currently prepared to meet the Creator of heaven and earth? Who do you say that Jesus is? What have you done with God's only Son? Ask God to show you the Gospel of His Son as you read Romans 10:5-13.

  _____

  _____

- "Therefore, if anyone is in Christ he is a new creation. The old has passed away; behold the new has come" 2 Corinthians 5:17.

  _____

  _____

- A prayer for help and change:

  _____

  _____

- Lord, help me to know you in new ways. I can't fight this illness or handle this challenge on my own anymore. Please change my heart to be more like Christ's. Come into my life. I turn it over to you. I'm sorry for trying to handle things in my own strength. I can do nothing without You. Please remove my pain and hurt and replace it with Your peace and joy. Your will be done, not mine. In Jesus' name, amen.

  _____

  _____

LETTER 3:

Mans' Medical Options

January 5, 2005

Dear brothers and sisters,

I wanted to update you on our recent visit to the stem cell transplant doctor in Dallas. This occurred on Monday at the UT Southwest Medical Center, with Dr. Robert Collins. He was most gracious and informative. He's highly respected in the North Texas area and comes recommended by all sources we've found.

The visit was not an uplifting one; it was a reality check. The doctor quickly reminded us that this cancer has no cure and will return. The stem cell will buy time and possibly extend my life, but it could also end my life quickly. The average life span for Multiple Myeloma patients is now five years, up from three years just a few years ago. Meaning that some die after one year while others die after ten, thus the five year average. No one knows which end of the scale I'll be.

He gave us three basic options to think about:

Option 1: "Auto" transplant where they would harvest my stem cells, treat me with chemo, and reinsert my stem cells back into my body. The positives to this method; less hard on the body and only reflects less than a two percent mortality rate caused from the transplant. The negatives are that I'd be reinserting my cancerous cells and a defective immune system back into my body, and the cancer would return in a shorter time frame.

Option 2: "Allo" transplant where related third party (one of my siblings) is used. You would come to Dallas and be given a shot that separates your stem cells from your bone marrow. They would then take blood from you as if you were donating, extract the stem cells from it and return the balance to you. I would have already been treated with chemo, and then I would have your stem cells inserted into my system. The positives are that cancer free stem cells will replace my cancer saturated ones. I will have a new immune system to fight my cancer. This method involves the hope of placing this cancer into remission, with the cancer being slower to return.

The negatives are that the procedure is higher risk to me and has a ten to twenty percent mortality rate within the first year. There is also a fifty percent risk that I'd develop the "graft vs. host disease" within the first few months following stem cell. This disease carries a fifteen to twenty percent mortality rate and/or has very debilitating side effects that could be with me the rest of my life.

Option 3: "Mini-Allo" transplant, where options one and two are both utilized, with option two following option one after two weeks. The positives involve less risk to me during stem cell. I'd still receive a new immune system, which would kill my old system off in time. The negatives involve a high risk of developing "graft vs. host disease."

As you can see, there are no clear cut answers to us at this point, but this will allow us to know if an "Allo" option is available. It appears that a stem cell transplant must occur soon with me, in that eighty percent of my bone marrow has been saturated with this cancer. They must destroy the cancer so my body can once again produce blood. The oral chemo I'm taking now has begun that process but can only help so much. The heavy chemo will complete it.

Our doctor feels the transplant will occur sometime in March. I appreciate your willingness to submit to this testing. I love each of you very much and will understand if you should not wish to subject yourself to this procedure.

With all my love, Bill

Points To Ponder

"The cross is rough, and it is deadly, but it is effective. It does not keep its victim hanging there forever."

A.W. TOZER

- Since God is "The Great Physician", as well as being infinitely wise in all things, we should be thankful regardless of what we do or do not receive in this life. If we have Christ, we have all we need both for time and eternity.

- Why are the Great Physician's hands better than man-made medical options?

- God knows what He's doing and always gives us what we need. When He takes us out into the desert, He stays with us through the trials. After all, His Spirit led His own Son into the wilderness of temptation (see Matthew 4:1 and Luke 4:1), as well as to the ignominy of the cross. He wants us to learn to depend solely on Him.

- "He forgives all my sins and heals all my diseases. He saves my life from the grave and loads me with love and mercy. He satisfies me with good things and makes me young again like the eagle" Psalm 103:3-5.

_____

_____

"If our Father permits a trial to come, it must be because the trial is the sweetest and best thing that could happen to us, and we must accept it with thanks from His dear hand. This does not mean, however, that we must like or enjoy the trial itself, but that we must like God's will in the trial."

HANNAH WHITALL SMITH

LETTER 4:

Second Opinion at Mayo Clinic

January 27, 2005

Dear family and friends,

It's been a month since I last communicated with you, so I wanted to catch you up on our recent visit to the Mayo Clinic, located in Rochester, MN. Our travel there was for the purpose of receiving a second opinion on my current protocol of treatment. The doctor assigned to my case is one of a team of ten doctors specializing in hematology. She studied my test results and proceeded to affirm that my current treatment program is the same program she'd recommend.

Treatment options are somewhat limited and case studies are few for multiple myeloma as a result of it being the least of all major cancers. It's never uplifting to be reminded that you have a terminal illness with a life expectancy of a few years, but I came away thankful that options are available that will possibly extend my life.

All of the Tsunami victims didn't have that option; they were taken in seconds or minutes. Our trip was profitable, and we have nothing but praise for the Mayo medical system in Rochester. We found it convenient, efficient, friendly and extremely professional.

The Mayo Clinic doctor stated that my current program could not continue indefinitely, and that the steroid regime would have to be suspended at some point in the near future. She recommended that I proceed with having my stem cells harvested while my protein count is low and store them for future use. She was most favorable to selecting the "Auto" (using my own stem cells vs. sibling stem cells) or perhaps a "double auto" where a month or so transpires between two different auto transplants. The safety of surviving such a transplant is high - ninety-eight percent versus a possible forty percent mortality rate within the first two years of a related third party transplant.

She stated that my cancer appeared to be an aggressive, fast-growing variety that has shown to respond quickly following a stem cell transplant. She would anticipate a 12 to 18 month period before the cancer would return should we select the "auto". The objective is to buy time, even if it's 12 to 18 additional months, in hopes that new drugs will be approved that might prolong my life further.

My family is doing well. We had the special treat of being accompanied to Rochester by our younger daughter, Kendra and our granddaughter, Marley. They were most helpful in keeping us entertained and running errands, etc. Our older daughter, Melissa, returns to us this weekend for another stay. She's been a blessing and has assisted us in incalculable ways.

Jan is the rock of the family. The Lord was kind to me for sending such a helpmate. Her strength and resolve have been greatly tested and challenged throughout these past two months, and she will emerge a stronger person as a result. My love and respect for her has only been enhanced. We know that much good comes from these trials in life.

My Relationship with Christ

Spiritually, we're resting in the Lord's strength. We continue to be diligent to do all things humanly possible to seek out the best care givers and care options, researching, and utilizing both conventional and some homeopathic solutions in fighting this cancer.

Ultimately we know that the Lord will direct our course. "Many are the plans in a man's heart, but it is the Lord's purpose that prevails" (Proverbs 19:21).

My greatest challenge is keeping in mind that this illness is not about me, never was, never will be. Yes, God is sanctifying me, disciplining me, readying me for His kingdom, but that is secondary to the primary reason for this illness - that He would be glorified through my illness.

I take comfort in knowing that I'm blessed by receiving His discipline. "Blessed is the man whom God corrects; so do not despise the discipline of the Almighty. For He wounds, but he also binds up; he injures, but His hands also heal" (Job 5:17-18). I've always grown most spiritually in times of hardship, not in times of prosperity.

I suppose that's why scripture says, "…we must go through many hardships to enter the kingdom of God…" (Acts 14:22). Only through hardships are we matured. God saved his chosen nation even though they remained disobedient and rebellious and not for their sake, but for His.

"For my own name's sake I delay my wrath; for the sake of my praise I hold it back from you, so as not to cut you off. See, I have refined you, though not as silver, I have tested you in the furnace of affliction. For my own sake, for my own sake, I do this. How can I let myself be defamed? I will not yield my glory to another" (Isaiah 48:9-11). There is no one else except Him who can be glorified.

Cancer has caused the attention to be shifted toward me. All calls, cards, letters are directed toward my illness, my cure – me! How blessed we've been by the continual love and concern exhibited through these various expressions. Yet, my Christian training teaches me to divert attention from myself and reflect it outwardly to the needs of others, ultimately deflecting all honor and glory to God.

Thus, it remains an ongoing challenge for me to not become self-absorbed with this added attention. In all honesty, I do not know how my illness will serve to glorify God. I only pray that it will and that I will keep "self" out of the picture. I pray as the Psalmist prayed, "Not to us, O Lord, not to us but to your name be the glory, because of your love and faithfulness" (Psalm 115:1).

Love, Bill

Points To Ponder

"The real problem is not why some pious, humble, believing people suffer, but why some do not."

C.S. LEWIS

- We must come to recognize the importance of embracing illness and anything else in this life with the perspective reflected in the following statement: "It's not about me, never was, never will be."

_____

_____

- The important thing is not that of knowing the immediate purpose for which one is suffering, but rather the eternal purpose of God to make His children more like Him. Most will not know in this life how their sufferings brought glory to God.

_____

_____

- The purpose in life is to enjoy God and to glorify Him in everything we do. How can you do this in your everyday life? Awareness, contentment with what He's given, appreciation, and by acknowledging Him in all the little details and giving Him thanks.

___

- God prunes us during trials so that we will bear much fruit. It is God's will in our lives for us to be sanctified, which is a process of Him molding us into His image. He does this until He's ready to call us home.

___

"His strength is made perfect, not in our strength, but in our weakness. Our strength is only a hindrance."

HANNAH WHITALL SMITH

LETTER 5:

Accepting Our Daily Bread

April 10, 2005

Dear friends and family,

It's been a rather lengthy period since I last forwarded an update concerning my condition and treatments. I will attempt to fill in the blanks from the past couple of months. Before I do, Jan and I wish to thank you for your prayers, letters, cards, encouragement, meals, and the love all of you continue to express. What a blessing you've been to us!

For the past four months, I've been on what's considered the "front-line" treatment for Multiple Myeloma patients. There are several different protocols that may be used. Mine consisted of Thalidomide and Dexamethazone. These are oral chemo drugs that have proven very successful in controlling the initial phase of the cancer, which has been the case for me.

The protein level in my blood has been reduced to a very low level, which indicates that the cancer is temporarily inactive. This has allowed my broken left humerus bone to heal and reattach much to the surprise of our orthopedic surgeon. She's very pleased with the progression.

Unfortunately, the two chemo drugs have taken a rather heavy toll on my body. The Dexamethazone steroid is very effective in fighting cancer, but it's most destructive in wasting your muscle tissue. I didn't realize just how destructive it could be. I ceased taking the steroid on March 25th and have mentally begun to come out of the "cloud" where mental confusion seemed to prevail most days.

My physical condition continued to deteriorate over the past four months to the point that I could not get up out of a chair or hold up my head without considerable effort. Thankfully, that phase of the treatment has now ceased, and for the past several days I've been able to regain some of my strength once again. It'll be a most arduous task to rebuild muscle tissue that's been destroyed for the past four months.

Stem Cell Transplant Update

Jan and I made a third visit to our stem cell transplant doctor at UT Southwestern in Dallas on April 4th.

We've decided to move forward with the stem cell transplant and wanted his opinion as to when and how to proceed. I didn't expect him to recommend the procedure until I regained some of the weight loss (24 pounds) and stamina. However, he does not wish to delay the procedure over four weeks and would prefer less time. Testing of vital organs will begin on April 14th. I will also have another bone marrow biopsy done.

These tests will confirm if I'm a candidate for the stem cell or not. I've failed to note that none of my siblings proved to be a match. The decision's been made to use my own stem cells rather than a third party due to the high risk it poses with the "graft vs. host" disease. Assuming I will qualify for the transplant, we will be in Dallas every day starting on May 5th for additional tests and shots.

Once all of the preliminary procedures cease, then the transplant will most likely occur within about four weeks, with the administering of high doses of chemo. Following the chemo, I'll be isolated in a private room with a special ventilation system for approximately three to four weeks. My immune system will have been totally destroyed during this time and a simple cold can cause a serious illness or even death, so visitation is highly restricted.

Jan will be allowed to stay in the room with me. Isolation will then continue at home for a period of time to allow the immune system to strengthen. It will take many months before my immune system is fully functioning again. If all goes well, Dr. Collins may follow up with some isolated radiation treatments to the areas where lesions (weak areas in my skeletal system) are detected.

Jan and I have much to be thankful for; myself especially, for the wonderful and loyal helpmate that my Lord and Savior chose for me almost thirty-one years ago. Jan's had to wear multiple hats for these past months and has suffered much anguish with godly grace during this time period. She fully understands the meaning of "for better or for worse" stated in our marriage covenant. She's doing better now that I seem to have turned the corner on this four month declination in my physical and mental state.

We're both so thankful for our local physician and the medical staff here in Granbury. We cannot begin to express our gratitude to them for all of the compassionate care and kindness shown to our family.

<u>Family News: A New Grandchild!</u>

We've also been blessed with the news that our younger daughter and son-in-law are expecting our second granddaughter. What a joy little Marley has been to us! We're awaiting another joyous gift from the Lord around Marley's third birthday in July. Kendra is handling the pregnancy very well, and we are excited, expectant grandparents.

Kendra and Marley accompanied us to the Mayo Clinic in January. It was great having them with us for support. We've also been blessed with a wonderful son-in-law who has made numerous trips from Austin to decorate and undecorate for Christmas, change filters, light bulbs, program the garage doors, etc. Jan always has a list for him when he comes. Most importantly, Kevin loves his family and has been a wonderful husband and father. We love him like a son and are very proud to have him in our family.

We are also thankful for our older daughter, Melissa, who was able to spend three months with me. She was such a blessing to both of us. She ran errands, made phone calls, cooked, kept me company, took me to doctor's appointments, etc. She recently relocated to Washington, D.C. and is back in the advertising business. She seems to really love the city. We're very proud of her, but we also miss her terribly. Having her with us made us appreciate her more.

My Relationship with Christ

My spiritual trial: I must confess that these past two months have been the most challenging mentally and spiritually. The Lord's remained faithful and has sustained me. Each morning I pray and ask for my daily manna. Not for food to eat, but spiritual sustenance. "Give us each day our daily bread" (Luke 11:3).

Many of those days I never closed the prayer but called out to Him throughout the day. If I ever began to question or doubt my Lord, I simply called out to Him, and He enlarged my faith and held it steadfast. He demands full dependence on Him. I know that I am to not be anxious about anything.

"Do not be anxious about anything, but in everything, by prayer and petition, with thanksgiving present your requests to God. And the peace of God, which transcends all understanding, will guard your hearts and your minds in Christ Jesus" (Philippians 4:6-7). He has most certainly sustained me with His peace.

Another test for me has been the lack of fellowship with my church family. I've truly missed this. It has been my weekly routine to spend Monday late afternoons,

Wednesday evenings, and Sunday morning with our church family.

The Lord has used that routine in my sanctification process as He continues to reshape and mold this sinful man. "As iron sharpens iron, so one man sharpens another" (Proverb 27:17). God has continually used others to encourage, challenge, rebuke, and support me, and I miss that greatly. Yet God is faithful and will sustain me spiritually during this difficult trial.

I've also failed spiritually in another area of this trial concerning joy. God not only tests us with trials but expects us to endure them, not as the world endures them with bitterness, anger and complaints. He expects Christians to do so with joy in their hearts.

"Be joyful always; pray continually; give thanks in all circumstances, for this is God's will for you in Christ Jesus" (1 Thessalonians 5:16-18). Regardless of our circumstances, pain or despair, we Christians should always exhibit joy, which only comes from the sustaining guidance of the Holy Spirit within us. Much too often I suppressed the glow of the Spirit and failed to reflect that joy.

I memorized a scripture several years ago that still amazes me each time I recite it because I pray God will teach me through this trial His joy, regardless of circumstances. "Though the fig tree does not bud and there are no grapes on the vines, though the olive crop fails and the fields produce no food, though there are no sheep in the pen and no cattle in the stalls, yet I will rejoice in the Lord, I will be joyful in God my Savior. The Sovereign Lord is my strength; he makes my feet like the feet of a deer, he enables me to go on the heights" (Habakkuk 3:17-19).

This man had lost all of his crops, all of his livestock, all that would physically sustain his family and himself, and instead of bitterness toward a sovereign God, this man rejoices and takes joy in the circumstances God has placed him in. I have much yet to learn. I pray God will enlarge my heart that I might exhibit His joy more fully through these trials.

Our Sovereign Lord and Savior is a wondrous creator and sustainer of all life, and He will continue to uphold Jan and me with His loving arms in our times of need. He will give us our daily manna – we need only ask.

In His caring and loving arms, I find my hope and joy.

Love, Bill and family

Points To Ponder

"We need never shout across the spaces to an absent God. He is nearer than our own soul, closer than our most secret thoughts."

A.W. TOZER

- Read the end of Proverbs 31 about the "Wife of Noble Character." As a wife or a spouse of a sick loved one, you will begin to understand the truth behind your wedding vows.

  _____

  _____

- How do illnesses and trials give your marriage a deeper dimension?

  _____

  _____

- As a spouse, what responsibilities do you have as a caregiver in God's eyes?

  _____

  _____

- Will you allow these challenging times to bring you closer to each other and to God by praying together and for each other, or will you allow selfishness to intervene and create a barrier between what God wants to show you?

_____

_____

- "When he heard this, Jesus said, 'This sickness will not end in death. No, it is for God's glory so that God's Son may be glorified through it'" John 11:4.

_____

_____

"Perhaps I am not meant to know the whys of this situation because God knows I don't have the capacity to understand the answer."

MAX LUCADO

LETTER 6:

The Lord is my Shepherd

May 1, 2005

Dear family and friends,

We'd like to update you on my most recent test results preceding the stem cell transplant. The purpose of these tests was to validate my physical stamina to undergo the transplant and to document the status of my cancer.

It's now been five months since my diagnosis of Multiple Myeloma, which ultimately destroys bone marrow and bone. I took Dexamethasone orally for four months and Thalidomide for almost five months. I'm presently taking neither.

The recent test results were most encouraging in that none of the tests reflected any signs of the cancer. The cancer is still present but has been suppressed to the point it's not measurable and is considered in remission at present. Jan and I have praised God for His tender mercies and for answering the many prayers.

Our oncologist wishes to proceed with the stem cell transplant. He feels it's our best hope in keeping the cancer in remission. The schedule is as follows: May 5th, surgically insert the Neostar (port) in my chest; May 6th-8th, neupogen shots to move stem cells out of bone marrow into the blood; May 9th-13th, harvest of stem cells; hope to get 10 million (enough for two transplants in case another is needed down the way); and May 18th, begin chemo and hospital isolation.

Hospital isolation should be for a period of two to three weeks, with isolation continuing at home for an additional month or two depending on how quickly my immune system returns. The literature claims recovery can vary between three to twelve months.

We remain thankful for all of your encouragement and prayers. Our doctors have followed a successful medical protocol, and we have confidence in their recommendations for treatment. Yet hope and faith rest with the Almighty, Sovereign God of our universe. He alone determines our fate. I know that I will not draw one more breath than He has ordained.

"From one man He made every nation of men, that they should inhabit the whole earth; and He determined the times set for them and the exact places where they should live" (Acts 17:26).

God has determined my exact time upon this earth. He could have taken me at the age of nine when I had spinal meningitis and was not expected to live. I have always considered that God gifted me every year beyond my ninth and feel blessed that He has allowed me to live for forty-five years beyond that time. How merciful our God is!

The book of Psalms has been a real blessing to my soul during these past five months. I read several daily prior to my prayer time and have memorized many as well. Psalm 23 is the most recent. What a comforting Psalm! It constantly reminds me that I'm led by God, not man. He guides my steps. He is my shepherd; I do not want for any other thing. He provides the most lush and tender grass for His flock (all my daily needs: physically and spiritually) and causes me to rest in His care.

Fear and anxieties have not conquered me because He continues to lead me by His calm Spirit restoring my soul. I take confidence that He will lead me in the paths of righteousness because He does so for His own glory – for His name sake. Even though I face death with this cancer, He has removed my fear by strengthening me through His Spirit. For my own good, He continues to discipline me with His rod and console and comfort me with His staff. What a wonderful God He is!

"The Lord is good, a refuge in times of trouble. He cares for those who trust in Him" (Nahum 1:7).

With the wonderful news concerning the status of my cancer, we give God all the praise. It is in Him that our hope and trust remain. May He be glorified in all things today and forever.

With love, Bill and family

Points To Ponder

"The best is yet to be."

John Wesley

- God demands full dependence on Him. Why do you think He wants us to rely on Him for strength instead of trying to be independent? He can give us all that we need. He also doesn't want us to get too attached to anyone or anything here. This earth and this life are temporary. Psalm 73:23-26 says, "Whom have I in heaven but You? And earth has nothing I desire besides You. My flesh and my heart may fail, but God is the strength of my heart and my portion forever."

  _____

  _____

- We are referred to in the Bible as sheep, while Jesus declares that He is our Good Shepherd (see John 10:14). Sheep are desperately dependent animals, because they are weak and need protection. Consider the fact that God is glorified in your dependence on Him. The Apostle Paul writes, "If I must boast, I will boast of the things that show my weakness" (2 Corinthians 11:30). "But he said to me, 'My grace is sufficient for you, for my power is made perfect in weakness. Therefore I will boast all the more gladly of my weaknesses, so that Christ's power may rest upon me" (2 Corinthians 12:9).

_____

_____

- How does God go about testing our faith through illness? Perhaps by isolation because He wants us all to Himself. He is jealous for our attention. God will sustain us fully during difficult trials like isolation. He may take us to the desert, but He doesn't leave us there alone. When we cry, He cries with us. That's comforting!

_____

_____

- We should exhibit joy in our trials because if we know Christ, then we are saved not *from* trials but *through* them to everlasting life.

_____

_____

- Slow down if necessary and spend more time getting to know the Lord.

_____

_____

- We can't always make sense out of our own illnesses or why God would allow our loved ones to suffer, but we do know that God does everything for His own good pleasure and glory, and that all He does is right. Deuteronomy 32:4 says, "The Rock, his work is perfect, for all his ways are justice. A God of faithfulness and without iniquity, just and upright is he." He only gives us what is best for us. Our finite minds are not able to comprehend His ways because they are not our ways (see Isaiah 55:8-9).

  _____

  _____

- To gain confidence in God's ways, what is our sword that holds all truth and encourages us? The Bible is full of people like Job, Paul and Jesus who have suffered far greater than we could ever begin to fathom. How do you find encouragement and hope in this? In Romans 15:4, Paul says that "whatever was written in former days was written for our instruction, that through endurance and through the encouragement of the Scriptures we might have hope."

  _____

  _____

- Be thankful in all things, especially trials. In them, God is making us look more like Him. "Count it all joy, my brothers, when you meet trials of various kinds, for you know that the testing of your faith produces steadfastness. And let steadfastness have its full effect, that you may be perfect and complete, lacking in nothing" (James 1:2-4).

_____

_____

"Sick believers may honor God as much by patient suffering as they can by active work. It often shows more grace to sit still than it does to go to and from and perform great exploits."

J.C. RYLE

LETTER 7:

Stem Cell Transplant

June 20, 2005

Dear family and friends,

Today marks four weeks since I entered Zale Lipshy in Dallas to receive my autologus stem cell transplant, and two weeks since my return home to Granbury. I can't tell you how wonderful it's been to be home rather than confined at the hospital. Zale Lipshy is a first class hospital facility with an exceptional stem cell team of professional caregivers. Yet confinement in any medical facility is not something I covet.

Ever since my diagnosis of Multiple Myeloma in December 2004, the stem cell transplant was proposed by my oncologist as an integral part of the recommended protocol in treating my cancer, and it was the treatment I most dreaded. I had read most of the available literature concerning the procedure, and it painted a rather bleak picture of possible outcomes. Sometimes I think I read too much! Thankfully, due to God's mercy, I didn't experience the severity of the side effects described in the literature.

Listed below are some of my journal notes during my hospital stay. I pray they will not bore you:

May 18, 2005: We arrived at the hospital at 8:00 a.m. and checked in. I was most anxious upon arrival and my mood somewhat somber. Paper work consumed the first hour, placing Jan and me in my room by 9:30 a.m. The nurses wasted no time in connecting me to an IV, and I received chemo (melphalan) at noon. The infusion lasted only 45 minutes, a shorter duration than I was expecting. This chemo must be potent! The nurses have increased my IV hydration, stating that this high rate is necessary to flush out the chemo so as to prevent damage to major organs. This heavy hydration will continue for twenty-four hours with hourly urination. This will be a fun night.

May 20, 2005: My medical care has been excellent. The entire staff is most attentive to my needs and remains focused on the smallest of health problems. They've informed and educated us as to what I can expect to experience throughout my stay.

My negative symptoms from the chemo haven't been severe yet. I don't feel well, and nausea remains my greatest obstacle to date. I've found that I must force myself to eat each meal; eating hurriedly before my stomach realizes it's being fed. Carter Blood Bank arrived around noon today to infuse approximately six million of my previously harvested stem cells.

I had twelve million stem cells harvested prior to this transplant, and Carter will maintain the balance of my stem cells for future use. Carter arrived with six plastic bags, each resembling blood transfusion bags frozen at a temperature of minus 191 degrees Celsius. They thawed each bag by submerging them in room temperature water.

I was warned that a strong smell, resembling either garlic or cream corn would be noticed immediately with the infusion of each bag of stem cells. I experienced a strong taste and the smell of creamed corn. Jan said it resembled burned cream corn to her.

The total process from the start to finish took approximately two hours, and I was informed that the cream corn smell would remain with me for a couple of days. The smell is from the preserving agent they used. The staff held a short ceremony calling today my "new" birthday – new life inserted into a poisoned body.

The chemo has been flushed from my system. However, the damage it has caused will not be fully experienced for several more days. Jan continues to ask how I feel, but it's difficult for me to describe. I do not feel well. It's a strange/odd sensation, a feeling I've never experienced before, and one I never wish to experience again.

I remain thankful for this treatment and know I should never dismiss the fact that I might someday have to repeat it. I continue to be grateful for mans' achievements in the field of medicine. Yet, I recognize that "The king's heart is in the hand of the Lord; he directs it like a watercourse wherever he pleases" (Proverbs 21:1).

Regardless of modern ingenuity, God continues to direct our affairs. I take comfort in that fact, "I will lie down and sleep in peace, for you alone, O Lord, make me dwell in safety" (Psalm 4:8).

May 23, 2005: During my quiet time yesterday, I prayed that the Lord would either bring forth a believer in my path or even an unbeliever who is interested in knowing more about Christ. I've missed Christian fellowship and long for the opportunity to share my faith with others.

May 24, 2005: The Lord was quick to answer my prayer. I've had the same nurse's assistant for the past two mornings. I noticed that her countenance the previous day was upbeat and pleasant, and she went about her tasks with a cheerful demeanor. This morning, while changing sheets on my bed, she began to praise God for her blessings.

She inquired as to whether or not I was a Christian. I responded in the positive, and we spent the next hour in delightful Christian fellowship. As it turns out, she also had been petitioning God to give her the courage to share her faith with me but had not done so the previous day out of fear she might be fired. She claimed the fear vanished this morning, and she felt at ease regardless of the consequences. Isn't it interesting the subtle manner in which God answered the prayers of two believers?

I'm thankful God hears my prayers and handles even the minutia of my daily affairs. What a comfort to know He leaves nothing to chance. "Are not two sparrows sold for a penny? Yet not one of them will fall to the ground apart from the will of your Father. And even the very hairs of your head are all numbered" (Matthew 10:29-30).

May 26, 2005: Today marks eight days into my anticipated fourteen day stem cell transplantation isolation. I'm now officially "neutropenic," meaning that I have a compromised immune system requiring isolation to prevent infections and illnesses, etc. The nurses post my blood test results daily in my room. This chart lists all key blood count results, such as red, white and platelet counts.

My white cell count is near zero currently; my red cell count is also extremely low, due to the destruction of my bone marrow, leaving me with a shortness of breath since red cells carry oxygen to my lungs. My platelet count is also in a downward spiral. My white cells fight off infections and diseases, while platelets cause clotting in case of internal injuries or cuts. My isolation here or at home must continue until my immune system is re-established, which may take a month or so.

My doctor reminded me today that my immune system is less than that of a new born infant and that all the childhood immunizations have vanished with the chemo. I must wait one year before I can once again be vaccinated for chicken pox, polio, etc. I must admit that my current condition has caused me to be somewhat anxious.

I realize that as a Christian, I should not be any more anxious today than any other day of my life because God is my ultimate sustainer. So why should I be fearful? Nonetheless, fear is present with me today, which reveals a real lack of faith. God's own word tells me to "Cast your cares on the Lord, and He shall sustain you; he will never let the righteous fall" (Psalm 55:22). In reality I should know that my daily existence is just as precarious when I'm healthy as when I'm sick. My anxiety is a sin – a lack of trust in the Lord.

May 30, 2005 - Memorial Day: No cookout for me today! I do not wish to eat anything, not even a hotdog, burger or steak. I've always enjoyed cooking out during the holidays, but I literally don't have the stomach for it. Today is my twelfth day in the hospital. The past three days have proven to be my most difficult due to a low grade fever, nausea and diarrhea.

I must confess that I really feel rotten. I must force myself to do everything, i.e., walk the hall, eat, stay up and out of bed (if possible), and to keep my mind on positive thoughts. This has been a most difficult period, and I call on my Lord frequently throughout the day to bolster my strength and fill me with His joy, peace and comfort. He's been faithful to do so.

A Humbling Experience

This early evening I've felt somewhat improved over the previous days. Hopefully the worst is behind me. I resorted to a rather sick form of entertainment, which Jan did not find as humorous as did I. I pushed back my hair from my forehead only to discover that numerous strands remained in my hand. Further tugging revealed that my hair was turning loose in abundance. So with Jan seated beside me, I proceeded to pull and pile hair in a neat stack between the two of us.

This continued for perhaps fifteen minutes, after which time she said, "I've just about had all I can stand of you pulling your hair out."

Thus ended my entertainment! A nurse was quickly summoned, and with barber shears in hand, she made quick work of my remaining hair. I hope bald is still "hip" because I certainly have a shiny head.

God is faithful to continue His training or His disciplining of this unworthy servant. Chemo has a way of stripping one of his/her vanity by disfiguring one both internally and externally – you are not the same. I needed this humbling because I am much too prideful and vain concerning my physical appearance. The Lord has taught me much thus far through this illness. A Christ-centered daily walk should always take precedence over my physical appearance.

"Have nothing to do with godless myths and old wives' tales; rather, train yourself to be godly. For physical training is of some value, but godliness has value for all things, holding promise for both the present life and the life to come" (1Timothy 4:7-8). I've always enjoyed a weekly workout routine, attempting to remain physically fit and have remained thankful for a full head of hair, though I must confess it has receded somewhat.

However, I often get out of balance, placing my physical conditioning and external appearance in front of godly pursuits. Thankfully, the Lord will not allow one to stray for long and has placed His hand of correction upon me in this area of sin in my life. He will do whatever it takes to keep His children humble.

"...This is the one I esteem: he who is humble and contrite in spirit and trembles at my word" (Isaiah 66:2).

I currently remain at home and have been given permission to wander some outside the neighborhood, visit family, go into my office, eat out upon occasion, and I was thrilled to attend church Sunday. What a blessing that was for Jan and me! We have a wonderful church family, and we've missed seeing them greatly.

My health remains stable, and my strength seems to improve with each week that passes. My oncologist does not anticipate placing me on what is termed a "maintenance regimen" of cancer drugs. At least not until such time as the cancer resurfaces. I can't tell you what a relief that news is to me, in that these drugs often have debilitating side effects. The Lord's been merciful to me and is worthy of all praise, honor, and glory.

Thank all of you for your continued encouragement in the form of cards, letters, emails, calls, visits, and thank you most for your prayers. Jan and I covet these so much.

I remain a servant only by His grace, Bill

Points To Ponder

"If you read history you will find that the Christians who did most for the present world were precisely those who thought most of the next. It is since Christians have largely ceased to think of the other world that they have become so ineffective in this world."

C.S. LEWIS

- "If then you have been raised with Christ, seek the things that are above, where Christ is, seated at the right hand of God. Set your minds on things that are above, not on things that are on earth. For you have died, and your life is hidden with Christ in God. When Christ who is your life appears, then you also will appear with him in glory" (Colossians 3:1-4).

  _____
  _____

- What do you consider positive reasons for the trials and tribulations of illness?

  _____
  _____

- How does illness help to reveal what is really in our hearts and who/what we truly love?

- Illness makes us reflect on death, which ultimately forces us to make a choice between hope and eternal life in Christ or despair and eternal death in hell. Either our faith gets stronger or it ceases to exist, and we are left alone.

- How does illness call us to encourage others? (Read 2 Corinthians 1:3-7)

- What good does it do to be anxious? Does this sin help? Why is it a lack of faith?

"Sickness is often one of the most humbling and distressing trials that can come upon man."

J.C. RYLE

LETTER 8:

Life after Stem Cell

October 2005

Dear family and friends,

"Praise be to the God and Father of our Lord Jesus Christ, the Father of compassion and the God of all comfort, who comforts us in all our troubles, so that we can comfort those in any trouble with the comfort we ourselves have received from God" (2 Corinthians 1:3-4).

My Heavenly Father has most certainly demonstrated His compassion and comfort to our family over these past several months. All praise and thanks be to Him! I returned home from the stem cell transplant on June 1st, approximately four months ago. The first couple of months I remained primarily isolated at home, though I was able to get out on a limited basis. Lack of stamina was my primary foe for the first several weeks, yet that has increased greatly.

I have a tendency to over-extend myself and prior to cancer could just push through my tired periods with my energy reserves. This is not the case now. Once my energy reserves have been spent, my engine stops. I must be careful not to find myself stranded out somewhere when this occurs, meaning I must plan ahead to rest prior to or immediately following an event.

My family is good to give me frequent lectures on this topic, and I'm grateful they have enough common sense to watch after me because there are many times I lack it. For example, I was over-exposed to children in July thinking it would not matter in that we were not in the cold and flu season. Children are my weakness. I love to be around them, to hug them and kid with them, so it's difficult for me to stay away. And, it's impossible for me to stay away from my grandchildren. I'm willing to run the risk to be with them.

My July exposure resulted in a cold, which is not bad in normal circumstances. Fever followed, and within a few days this led to a late night visit to the ER in Dallas with my doctors intending to hospitalize me for a few days. Thankfully my fever broke following the infusion of two separate high potency broad-spectrum antibiotics by IV in the ER. A small illness can lead to major consequences when you have a compromised immune system. I have to continuously remind myself of that fact!

That one incident has been the only major health setback I've experienced thus far. My immune system will remain suppressed for most of this year according to my oncologist, although the blood work continues to show improvement. I will be able to take my childhood immunization shots again around June of next year.

My most recent monthly checkup, which occurred this past week, did not reflect any presence of cancer. I'm tested bi-monthly for the presence of protein in my blood and urine. An elevated protein reading means my cancer has returned. My most recent test revealed no detectable trace of protein. My doctors would classify me as in remission from my cancer.

The doctors know that the cancer remains; it's just in hiding. It can return at any time, but on average it returns one year following stem cell. I remain content with whatever develops, yet I'd be lying to say it does not concern me and cause me worry upon occasion. Fortunately, these occasions are few and short in duration.

God's always been merciful to comfort me when I call out to Him to release me from the anxiety of cancer's return or the nearness of death. What a wondrous God we serve! I know that He will never leave me nor forsake me in times of trouble. He has proven that endlessly throughout my illness. I know He is present when I call out to Him for help, and He carries me through my trials.

I recently read a quote from a Puritan writer concerning Abraham who departed his homeland at an old age into an unknown country out of obedience to God. "Abraham went out, not knowing whither he went; but he did know with whom he went." I do not compare myself to Abraham, but I fully understand his confidence to go anywhere and do anything because of God's promise of providential care for His children.

I dread the return of my cancer but do not fear it. I trust that my God will not give me more than I can bear whenever that time comes. If I've learned anything in this struggle with cancer, it's my dependence upon my heavenly Father. All flesh ultimately fails to bring the kind of comfort needed during these life threatening times in our lives, only our Abba Father can comfort us during those times—praise be to Him!

Jan and the girls continue to rally around me, scolding me at times, but mostly encouraging me with loving gestures of kindness. This has also been true of our extended family, church family, and friends. What a blessing your prayers, cards, emails and letters have been to our family, and we remain profoundly grateful. We've felt your prayers. We would ask that you allow us the privilege of praying for you and your family as well. Please let us know your prayer concerns so that we can lift you and your family up during our daily devotional time.

With my health improving I've been able to return to most church and work duties. My hours have been curtailed but continue to expand as my health improves. Just prior to stem cell I divested myself of one business and cut back in some of my other business endeavors, with the overriding intent being to decrease my business activities and increase my service to God. That still remains my hope and desire. It's my prayer that His work and not my own will consume the majority of my remaining time on this earth.

I will close this letter with Psalm 30:10-12. "Hear, O Lord, and be merciful to me; O Lord, be my help. You turned my wailing into dancing; you removed my sackcloth and clothed me with joy, that my heart may sing to you and not be silent. O Lord my God, I will give you thanks forever."

God has been so kind and merciful to my family and me over this past year, and I remain thankful for this illness. It has served to sanctify my walk, to draw family and friends closer, has caused me to reprioritize my time, and redirect my focus on more important matters. And most importantly, the illness has caused me to praise Him endlessly for He and He alone has, "turned my wailing into dancing, removed my sackcloth and clothed me with joy." How could I not give Him thanks forever?

In the love of our Savior, Bill

Points To Ponder

"God cannot give us a happiness and peace apart from Himself, because it is not there. There is no such thing."

C.S. LEWIS

- Psalm 73:25-26 says, "Whom have I in heaven but you? And there is nothing on earth that I desire besides you. My flesh and my heart may fail, but God is the strength of my heart and my portion forever." Reflect upon the fact that your flesh and your heart will fail you, but if the Lord Jesus is your Savior, then He will be your strength and your portion forever.

  _____
  _____

- How has illness or other trials in your own life caused your priorities to change in order to glorify God?

  _____
  _____

- What things have changed, and what have you learned as a result?

  _____
  _____

- 2 Corinthians 1:9 says, "Indeed, we felt that we had received the sentence of death. But that was to make us rely not on ourselves but on God who raises the dead."

  _____

  _____

- How can you choose to be thankful for your illness?

  _____

  _____

- What might keep you from praising Him during challenges?

  _____

  _____

"I want to know God's thoughts; the rest are details."

ALBERT EINSTEIN

LETTER 9:

The Cancer Returns

January 2006

Dear family and friends,

It was January of last year that I penned the first update concerning my illness. At that time I could not fathom how I might survive the year, much less have my life return to near normalcy. I'd just been diagnosed in the latter stages of multiple myeloma, with eighty percent penetration into my bone marrow.

Upon admission into the hospital, doctors discovered that I was deficient of almost half my blood supply. Besides destroying my blood production, the cancer had partially eaten through my left humerus bone and had caused the breakage of three ribs due to bone lesions.

In the early part of January, I was readmitted to the hospital with a blood clot in my right lung. By the end of the four months of oral chemo, I'd lost 30 pounds and resembled an emaciated prisoner of war. It was difficult to hold my head upright. Any kind of physical exertion was most strenuous and exhausting.

I was not a pretty sight to behold, and my exterior appearance was superior to my interior condition. I battled daily to keep my emotional and spiritual temperaments in check. Thankfully the Lord stopped my physical decline as of April 2005, enabling me to undergo a stem cell transplant in May. My physical condition has steadily improved since that time.

My purpose in sharing this is not for sympathy or pity, but rather that you might focus on God's mercy in restoring my health. What a wondrous and merciful God we serve! He took me to death's door so that I could see it, taste it, and smell it, and left me there for months before returning my health.

Being that near death has forever changed my life for the better. Eliphaz said to Job, "For he (God) wounds, but he also binds up; he injures, but His hands also heal" (Job 5:18). God chose to injure me, then to heal me, and all for His express purpose.

In all honesty, I have no idea for what purpose God has spared my life, but I can assure you that I'm thankful and will sing His praises for all of my remaining days.

The Cancer Returns

Many of you prayed for my healing this past year, and I thank you for your devotion to prayer. God glorifies Himself through our prayers. I've found it difficult to know how to pray. I've selfishly prayed for healing, yet I've also asked that His will be done and not my own.

And if He chooses not to change my circumstances, then I pray that He will give me contentment with my circumstances. He's shown me that I should not be anxious or worry about that which I cannot change. "Who of you by worrying can add a single hour to his life?" (Matthew 6:27). I have not mastered the sin of worry but am much closer now than before my illness.

My last report to you was in October of 2005, and I reported then that my cancer was non-detectable and my blood work was improving with each visit. My status remains the same with this exception: my cancer is now detectable. There was no trace of protein in my blood in October.

That changed in November when my protein test revealed a reading of 0.14. The protein test is my doctor's method of determining the level of activity for my cancer. My December blood tests showed a protein reading of 0.40, thus my cancer is returning. To give you a comparison of my protein reading today compared to when I was first diagnosed with cancer in November of 2004, my protein reading then was extremely high at 6.90. I'm hopeful that my doctor will allow more time before placing me on new chemo medications. The available drugs to combat my disease are limited, and their effectiveness varies widely by individual as do the side effects.

My blood protein increase is God's way of reminding me that I have an incurable cancer, and that my time here as a sojourner will be limited. I feel He is telling me to redeem my time, use it wisely, and to spend little time maintaining my kingdom and much time in the furtherance of His.

He's given me renewed hope, allowed me additional time with my family and friends, has given me the opportunity to celebrate my second granddaughter's birth, and the privilege of spending Thanksgiving in Colorado with my family. What a blessing these past few months have been.

Jan and I remain thankful for all that the Lord has brought our way this past year, including my illness. God has used this illness to further sanctify us and prepare us to spend eternity with Him. We've learned to be grateful for the smallest blessings and to appreciate each and every day He's given us.

May God's kind providence shine upon you and your family this coming year.

By His strength and for His glory, Bill

Points to Ponder

"I believe in Christianity as I believe that the sun has risen: not only because I see it but because by it I see everything else."

C.S. LEWIS

- How are you preparing to spend eternity with the Lord?

  _____

  _____

- Hebrews 11:13-16 says, "These all died in faith, not having received the things promised, but having seen them and greeted them from afar, and having acknowledged that they were strangers and exiles on the earth. For people who speak thus make it clear that they are seeking a homeland. If they had been thinking of that land from which they had gone out, they would have had opportunity to return. But as it is, they desire a better country, that is, a heavenly one. Therefore God is not ashamed to be called their God, for he has prepared for them a city."

  _____

  _____

- Have you considered what you will leave behind as your legacy?

  _____

  _____

- Are there people you need to forgive, make amends with, or anger and bitterness you need to let go of and surrender to God? What is stopping you from doing this today?

_____

_____

"He who sides with God cannot fail to win in every encounter; and whether the result is joy or sorrow, failure or success, death or life, we may under all circumstances join in the apostle's shout of victory, 'Thanks be unto God,' which always causeth us to triumph in Christ!"

HANNAH WHITALL SMITH

LETTER 10:

Contentment in God's Will

May 4, 2006

Dear family and friends,

It is the evening of the day my sweetheart married me 32 years ago. What a blessing Jan has been to me! I was an unbeliever when I married her and remained such for the first twelve years of our marriage. What misery I gave her about her faith during those years. But God, in His great providence and mercy, pulled me out of that great darkness into His wonderful light, changing a stony heart into one of flesh. What a miracle!

Concerning my health; my last update was forwarded in January of this year wherein I stated that my cancer was once again visible due to the heightened reading of protein in my blood. Shortly after sending that update my protein jumped considerably, causing my oncologist to place me back on an oral chemo protocol or treatment program in mid-March.

I'm currently on two oral chemo drugs: Thalidomide and Prednisone. Since March 15th of this year, I've been on one half of last year's dosage. However, we received a call from my oncologist today claiming that my protein count has not diminished following six weeks of treatment and has continued to rise. They now want to double my dosage on the Thalidomide.

This will increase the side effects but hopefully will bring the protein count back into an acceptable range. Most of my blood test reports in recent months have shown a decline in blood production, reflecting the renewed cancer activity. This reduced blood level led to rather heavy fatigue. I was given a Procrit shot this past week to boost the production of my red blood cells, and that seems to have helped with my stamina and strength.

I've hesitated to send out updates because so many others have far greater concerns. Yet several have asked that I forward an update so they might know how best to pray for my family and me. Jan and I selfishly pray for healing but rest contently in whatever our Lord brings our way.

This illness has shown both of us that He will not forsake us in times of trouble but will remain faithful to give us an extra measure of strength when it is needed. He never promised us health, wealth, and prosperity upon conversion. Just the opposite in fact. "...We must go through many hardships to enter the kingdom of God" (Acts 14:22). I continue to pray as the Psalmist, "Show me, O Lord, my life's end and the number of days; let me know how fleeting my life is. You have made my days a mere handbreadth; the span of my years is as nothing before you. Each man's life is but a breath" (Psalm 39:4-5).

I reflect on this Psalm frequently just to remind myself of the brevity of life; it is but a breath when compared to eternity. My Lord continues to remind me that my time has been shortened and to use it wisely. Unfortunately, I fail miserably in this area, but I can assure you it remains on my heart daily.

Jan and I remain optimistic and hopeful. We experience God's comfort, joy, and peace on a daily basis. He continues to sustain us with His daily bread and makes us thankful for each and every day we are given. Thank you for your prayers. May all praise and honor be to our Lord and Savior Jesus Christ! Love, Bill

Points To Ponder

"God's purpose for my life was that I have a passion for God's glory and that I have a passion for my joy in that glory, and that these two are one passion."

JONATHAN EDWARDS

- Be thankful. Count your blessings. 1 Thessalonians 5:18 tells us to "give thanks in all circumstances; for this is the will of God in Christ Jesus for you."

_____

_____

- Consider some situations or occurrences concerning which you tend to be ungrateful. Ask God to create in you a heart of thanksgiving.

_____

_____

- God will not leave us in times of trouble but will give us extra strength for what we need to overcome it. Hebrews 13:5 says "...for he has said, 'I will never leave you nor forsake you.'" (See also Ephesians 3:14-20.)

- Paul says in Philippians 4:11-13, "I have learned in whatever situation I am to be content. I know how to be brought low, and I know how to abound. In any and every circumstance, I have learned the secret of facing plenty and hunger, abundance and need. I can do all things through him who strengthens me."

_____

_____

- Psalm 103:15-16 says, "As for man, his days are like grass, he flourishes like a flower of the field; the wind blows over it and it is gone, and its place remember it no more."

_____

_____

"We can only walk this path by 'looking continually unto Jesus,' moment by moment. And if our eyes are turned away from Him to look upon our sin and our weakness, we shall leave the path at once."

HANNAH WHITALL SMITH

LETTER 11:
Near Death with Spinal Meningitis

August 4, 2006

Dear family and friends,

I've been home for two full days from my hospital stay at Zale Lipshy. What a blessing to be home! Jan and I do not know where to begin expressing our gratitude. The outpouring of love and help from our immediate family, church family, and friends has one again overwhelmed us.

I returned home to find that family and friends had moved us out of our old home and into a new one, and not only moved us but stored away items in our attic, set up our kitchen, book shelves, etc. The list goes on, and what a joy it was to walk into a new home already put together. We thank you!

We wish to thank our children and our son-in-law for their love and support through this. Their help was beyond measure before, during and following my illness. Most of my siblings came by as did Jan's family. Many friends also came by.

Unfortunately, I've been told by my children and spouse that my Christian deportment was somewhat deficient during my stay in the ICU. I have yet to hear all the stories but do wish to apologize for having an over-active tongue. I can remember a few faces, yet do not remember any conversations, which apparently is a good thing.

Our Christian faith teaches, "A man of knowledge uses words with restraint, and a man of understanding is even-tempered. Even a fool is thought wise if he keeps silent, and discerning if he holds his tongue" (Proverbs 17:27-28).

What about my bacterial spinal meningitis prognosis? Jan took me to the Hood County hospital on July 26th with a severe headache. They administered morphine to me twice while waiting to transport me to our oncologist.

I was placed in Zale Lipshy, the same hospital I had my stem cell transplant in May 2005. I don't remember much that occurred until July 30th. I was able to leave the hospital on August 2nd due to the IV technology called a "pick line."

This line was surgically placed in my left arm on the day of my departure and enables me to receive pressurized antibiotics twice daily with the assistance of Community Care, a home health firm here in Granbury, and my family who assists. I receive these drugs twice daily over a period of an hour and a half. This routine will continue for fourteen days.

I have some damage from the meningitis. My left eye ceased to function for a couple of days during my semiconscious state. It appears to be coming back but is lazy and drags when I attempt quick eye movement on reading. I've also lost the hearing out of my right ear, but it may return over time. Jan and I feel most fortunate that nothing worse occurred. Many lose their lives to this disease or suffer much worse damage than I did.

My recovery will be slow. We asked Dr. Collins about what we can expect during my recovery, and he stated the following:

- that my immune system will remain low
- recommended that I stay isolated, with limited visitation
- recuperation will be slow, so be patient

You know how difficult this will be for Jan and me. We both love our family and friends dearly, and to be isolated is most difficult for us. So we thank you for your kindness and expressions of love by sending cards and letters of encouragement. Many have brought meals, and we currently have an abundance of food thanks to that kindness.

How are we spiritually? Thanks to our Lord and Savior Jesus Christ we remain steadfast. We've kept our eyes fixed on our Savior who is, "the author and perfecter of our faith," (Hebrews 12:2) and "have cast our cares on the Lord, and He has sustained us" (Psalm 55:22).

We observe God's providential hand in all things, especially our difficulties, and so we thank Him for the deepening of our faith. Jan and I believe that these illnesses are not random but designed for the good of His children. "Consider it pure joy, my brothers, whenever you face trials of many kinds, because you know that the testing of your faith develops perseverance" (James 1:2-3).

All of my illnesses and recovery have produced increased steadfastness and comfort. It's been difficult yet comforting. He makes us rest more and more upon Him. We are thankful for all He brings our way because we benefit long term.

What about my cancer? I'm still battling a spike in my protein. It jumped to 6.24 just prior to my most recent protocol change during the latter part of July. The 6.24 protein count is just slightly lower than when first diagnosed in November 2004 at 6.9. One of the side effects of the new drug protocol is neutropenia, an extremely low white blood cell level which helps to fight infections.

We realize our responsibility to take every human precaution to remain healthy, and we are making every effort to do so. Yet we know our Heavenly Father directs the ultimate time of our departure. "…All the days ordained for me were written in your book before one of them came to be" (Psalms 139:16).

Thank you again for your support and love. May the Lord continue to uphold your household with His tender loving hand. We continue steadfast because He sustains us.

Love, Bill

Points To Ponder

"A man can no more diminish God's glory by refusing to worship Him than a lunatic can put out the sun by scribbling the word, 'darkness' on the walls of his cell."

C.S. LEWIS

- God's providential hand is in all things, especially our difficulties. This fact alone should deepen our faith and quiet our doubts.

_____

_____

- Illnesses are designed by God for good, to test our faith, develop character and perseverance. We glorify God by believing in His promises.

_____

_____

- Psalm 56:13 says, "For you have delivered my soul from death, yes, my feet from falling, that I may walk before God in the light of life."

_____

_____

- In Psalm 23:4, David declares, "Even though I walk through the valley of the shadow of death, I will fear no evil, for you are with me; your rod and your staff, they comfort me."

- Rest in Jesus. Ask Him to wrap His arms around you and rock you to sleep or curl up at His feet for peace and comfort.

- Psalm 116:7 says, "Return, O my soul, to your rest; for the Lord has dealt bountifully with you." Do you realize that regardless of the degree of pain or pleasure in your life, the Lord has dealt with you bountifully?

"God allows pain, sickness and disease not because He loves to vex man, but because He desires to benefit man's heart, and mind and conscience, and soul, to all eternity."

J.C. Ryle

LETTER 12:

A State of Thankfulness

December 12, 2006

Dear family and friends,

Our family would like to wish yours a happy and prosperous Christmas holiday season. We pray that your health remains good and your eyes remain focused on the real reason we celebrate Christmas.

It's so subtle how the world continuously attempts to remove Christ from Christmas, by either using the shortcut spelling reference of X-mas, or in referring to this time of the year as Happy Holidays. The world might succeed in removing the external references, but for the children of God, the world can never remove the internal love we possess.

How thankful we remain for that assurance, "All that the Father gives me will come to me, and whoever comes to me I will never drive away" (John 6:37).

"My sheep listen to my voice; I know them, and they follow me. I give them eternal life, and they shall never perish; no one can snatch them out of my hand" (John 10:27). What a blessed assurance we have from our Savior!

All remains well with our family. Kevin, Kendra and the girls, Marley and Tessa, live within ten miles of our home, and we have the privilege and blessing of spending time with them frequently. Marley is now four and loves anything to do with princesses, the color pink and mermaids, while Tessa at seventeen months loves dancing and giving kisses – activities that seem to somewhat bother her father. What sweethearts those two are!

Melissa remains well and deeply planted in Washington, D.C. She's working for the GSA (General Services Administration), which is like the landlord for the federal government and is extensive in the real estate services they provide nationwide. She finds herself doing various types of communications for the PBS (Public Buildings Service) Commissioner at GSA - writing speeches and working with the media, so this compliments her journalism degree rather well.

Jan remains my rock and wonderful helpmate. What a blessing she remains to all of our family. She seems to never stop. She's an industrious woman who rises early and works late. I've had the privilege of being her husband for these past 32 years. The Lord is kind and merciful!

My health remains good, and we are thankful. My bout with spinal meningitis this past July was difficult, but I've fully recovered from it with only some hearing loss in my right ear, which gives me an excuse to have selective hearing. I've only had one cold since my return home from the hospital in August. I remain somewhat secluded due to my low immune system.

I'm currently taking Revlimid and Dexamethasome for my Multiple Myeloma treatment, and one of the side effects is a lowered immune system. However, I've been able to participate in some of our church services, able to go into work for short periods of time, occasionally eat out, and basically live a normal life. Some of my days are really low energy days, so I remain home on those days and rest between activities and work.

Jan and I attempt to end each evening thanking God for the good things He has brought our way for that one day. It's been amazing what He continues to reveal to us when we are diligent to thank Him.

We take each day one at a time, knowing that our strength and hope remains with Him. He continues to comfort us on our down days and gives us hope. Our faith continues to be tested and strengthened. There always seems to be a new health challenge, which we continue to lay at His feet and not attempt to bear the burden ourselves.

We walk by faith in Him, knowing that we are responsible to do all within our power to maintain good health, yet recognizing it is our Lord that will direct my ultimate path.

"The Lord is good, a refuge in times of trouble. He cares for those who trust in Him" (Nahum 1:7). "Let us fix our eyes on Jesus, the author and perfecter of our faith..." (Hebrews 12:2).

We remain steadfast in His love by His sovereign will, Bill

Points To Ponder

"I gave in, and admitted that God was God."

C.S. LEWIS

- Make it a habit to thank God for the good things He's given you. God turns the ugly into something beautiful. He refines us by fire.

  _____

  _____

- What are you thankful for now that you weren't able to see the beauty in before?

  _____

  _____

- Ask God to reveal things to you giving you insight, understanding and wisdom and the ability to praise Him no matter what.

  _____

  _____

- Take one day at a time, becoming dependent on Him by asking for help and guidance, understanding that your strength and hope remain in Him.

_____

_____

"I am not going from a prison to a palace. I have finished my work, and am now going to receive my wages."

CHRISTOPHER LOVE

LETTER 13:

"What Condition My Condition Is In"

February 10, 2007

Dear Elders, Staff and Deacons at Grace Community Church,

I realize that this 70's song somewhat dates me, or perhaps you were just born too late to appreciate the depth and richness of the songs like, "What Condition My Condition Is In."

Jan and I spent Thursday at the UTSW clinic for blood work, evaluation, and to receive two units of blood. My doctor decided that, given the fact that my SPEP protein test results once again reflect an increased blood protein level, and the current protocol does not seem to be working that it would be necessary to begin a new regimen.

He called it "bridging the gap," hoping to find something to hold me for a few months until a new trial arrives. The new trial medication is thought to be superior to the others now available, so he is excited to get me into trial.

We returned to Dallas on Friday for a nuclear heart stress test to see if my heart will withstand the new chemo protocol. I suppose that it did in that I'm still here. They never mentioned the results. We must be in Dallas early Monday to have a port installed into my chest. It will be for the purpose of administering the chemo.

The nurse told us on Friday that should the chemo accidentally get out of the tubing and beneath the skin that it would totally destroy all the skin it touches. Of course I'm sitting there thinking, "and you are about to put that into my veins and send it to my heart?" It sure makes one think.

I will be given my first chemo on Monday afternoon and one additional chemo each day following, with Friday being my last day. Each new chemo will be given using a battery pack over a 24 hour period. The two weeks following the chemo I'll have blood tests only to measure the impact of the chemo on my body, then back to chemo the third week. The cycle then repeats itself.

I do not know how I'll respond to this new protocol, but I do know that I have One who will sustain, strengthen and comfort me through any of my trials. I must confess that this treatment concerns me more than the others, but there will most probably be a time that no options exist without divine intervention.

I don't know when or if this might happen. I don't allow myself to focus on such things and remain aware of His love and mercy that is given to me daily. It is always there. May we all bring glory to Him in how we live our lives, may we redeem our time and spend it wisely.

"Therefore, do not worry about tomorrow, for tomorrow will worry about itself. Each day has enough trouble of its own" (Matthew 6:34).

If we worry about tomorrow, it will rob us of our joy today. I love each and every one of you. Thank you for your continued care, service and encouragement to our flock.

Love, Bill

Points To Ponder

"The enjoyment of God is our highest happiness."

JONATHAN EDWARDS

- What condition is your spiritual life in?

  _____

  _____

- How has your own illness or a loved one's brought your closer to Christ? Or has it caused you to turn away? He always corrects our paths when we repent and ask for help. God is full of mercy and quick to forgive.

  _____

  _____

- What are God's promises to His children? Dwell, ponder, remember these when you are in pain. Focus only on His truths, not on what or how you feel.

  _____

  _____

- The Lord loves us and is mighty to save.

_____

_____

"To go to heaven, fully to enjoy God, is infinitely better than the most pleasant accommodations here."

JONATHAN EDWARDS

LETTER 14:

Testing the Genuineness of Our Faith

June 10, 2007

Dear family and friends,

I'd like to update you on what has occurred with my illness since January 2007. I've been somewhat remise in keeping you informed of the progression of my cancer. On May 23rd I went in for a regular doctor's check-up, and they discovered I needed to be hospitalized for pneumonia.

During this stay they did multiple tests to help fight the pneumonia and to measure the progress of my cancer. The doctors did a bone marrow aspiration to see to what degree the cancer had penetrated my bone marrow and discovered that the majority of my bone marrow is saturated with myeloma cells. This test indicated I'd have to begin a new treatment series because the current one was not working.

The new treatment will be using the drug Velcade, which attacks the Multiple Myeloma from a different perspective. It will be the fourth protocol I've used since January. At this point only one of those protocols helped to slow the progression of the cancer. We should know if the Velcade is working by the end of June.

Currently my body does not have a natural immune system and does not produce blood or platelets. The new protocol must take effect before my body will be able to produce its own blood.

Our faith still remains very strong because, regardless of these setbacks, we rest in the strength of our Lord. Yes, there are times we are somewhat discouraged, yet God never fails to sustain us through his strength. God does not send illness to harm us but to train us, and we are thankful He considers us worthy for this test.

I know that God seeks His own glory in our infirmities. "See, I have refined you, though not as silver; I have tested you in the furnace of affliction. For my own sake, for my own sake, I do this. How can I let myself be defamed? I will not yield my glory to another" (Isaiah 48:10-12).

God is also testing the genuineness of my faith with this cancer. "In this you greatly rejoice, though now for a little while you may have had to suffer grief in all kinds of trials. These have come so that your faith – of greater worth than gold, which perishes even though refined by fire – may be proved genuine and may result in praise, glory and honor when Jesus Christ is revealed" (1 Peter 1:6-7).

Whether I triumph or succumb to this illness rests with the Lord, and Jan and I remain content with His election. May He be glorified by my illness – all praise be to a Holy, Sovereign God.

On behalf of our family, Jan and I wish to thank you for your support, encouragement, love, care, calls, visits, meals, trips to the doctor's office, and most of all your continued prayers.

In Christ alone, we remain hopeful, Bill

Points To Ponder

"We see life differently when we realize that death isn't a wall but a turnstile; a small obstacle that marks a great beginning."

RANDY ALCORN

- God doesn't send illness to harm us but to train us. Be thankful when he considers us worthy for this test and rest in His promise that He never gives us more than we can handle.

_____

_____

- How has the genuineness of your faith been tested? With illness or something else?

_____

_____

- How do we glorify God through our illness or trials?

_____

_____

"If you are a Christian, you are not a citizen of this world trying to get to heaven; you are a citizen of heaven making your way through this world."

VANCE HAVNER

LETTER 15:

In Christ Alone

June 17, 2007

Dear friends and family,

I realize that an update has just been forwarded to you in the past couple of weeks, but we have a praise we'd like to share. Many times I'm guilty of praying and then failing to praise my Lord and Savior for answering my prayers. So many of you have been faithful to pray for Jan and me, and we remain most thankful.

Our prayer is that He brings my cancer into remission or cure, yet we also pray that His Will be done and that He be honored in my life or my death.

Our Thursday visit to the oncologist revealed that my SPEP protein level has fallen rather dramatically: from 6.0 (it was 6.9 when I was first diagnosed) down to 3.55. These numbers may not mean anything to many of you in that you do not follow them as closely as we do.

That drop was a huge movement in my protein which reveals that my cancer is decreasing and that the new medication is working. My oncologist would like to see my SPEP at 1.00 or less. The reading was after taking Velcade for a period of two weeks as a lone drug. The oncologist is planning to add additional chemo drugs should Velcade begin to lose its lone effectiveness.

Where has this news led us but straight to our knees in praise and gratitude to our Sovereign Lord and Savior? Oh, what a comforting feeling it is to rest in the care of a loving God. He truly continues to amaze us. Most of the high-powered drugs have now been used by my oncologist. Various combinations of previously used drugs still remain as options. Velcade has not been used until now because it requires frequent trips to Dallas for either the chemo or blood transfusions, and it greatly reduces all of my blood counts, leaving me to constantly battle neutropenia (no immune system).

Our oncologist continues to warn me of my exposure to people, thus I will remain somewhat secluded until my blood counts rise. He said visitors are allowed, just insure they're not ill and keep the visits at a reasonable time limit. Not tough advice for most, but extremely hard for someone like me who loves being with and visiting with people. Thus, you will need to help me limit my visiting.

We remain awed and overcome by our Savior's love and kindness with this new reading. What a magnificent God we serve! And though we know all drugs eventually cease to be effective, we also know we worship a God where all things are possible.

Our God does not need doctors or anyone else to accomplish His deeds, yet He continues to use man to accomplish many of these tasks. God's victory over His foes, whether an armed enemy, disease, etc. is accomplished using few and not many, so that He may receive the glory and not us.

Take Gideon as an example. "The Lord said to Gideon, 'You have too many men for me to deliver Midian into their hands. In order that Israel may not boast against me that her own strength has saved her, announce now to the people, 'Anyone who trembles with fear may turn back and leave Mount Gilead'" (Judges 7:2). God goes on to reduce Gideon's forces to 300 to combat the thousands of Midianites, all to prove that it is He who gets the victory and not Israel.

It appeared that all of the medications were going to fail in stopping the progression of this cancer, and we were resolved to that reality. Yet God has taken a few of the remaining drugs to reverse my cancer and all for His name's sake. How can Jan and I not proclaim, "Since you are my rock and my fortress, for the sake of your name lead and guide me" (Psalm 31:3)?

In the love and strength of the Lord Jesus Christ, Bill and Jan

Points To Ponder

"I wonder many times that ever a child of God should have a sad heart, considering what the Lord is preparing for him."

SAMUEL RUTHERFORD

- "O God, quicken to life every power within me, that I may lay hold on eternal things. Open my eyes that I may see; give me acute spiritual perception; enable me to taste Thee and know that Thou art good. Make heaven more real to me than any earthly thing has ever been. Amen." A.W. Tozer

- With God all things were possible.

- God is the "Great Physician" and He will choose to heal us when and if it pleases Him.

- We must rely on Christ alone.

　

　

- We should praise God regardless of good or bad news. If we are His children, it's always good news because we have eternal life.

　

　

- Paul learned to be content in all circumstances, whether he was hungry, poor, beaten, ridiculed, imprisoned, suffering or dying. He trusted God and longed to do His will.

　

　

- What if in the midst of imploring God to remove your illness or trial, you heard Him say, "My grace is sufficient for you"?

- Is it fair to question God if He saves us from hell and nothing more? Do we dare complain about an earthly diminishing body when we know heavenly treasures await?

___

___

"I am still in the land of the dying; I shall be in the land of the living soon."

JOHN NEWTON

PROMISES:

The Rainbows God Sent

By Melissa Wren Brown

On August 16, 2007, the night before my dad died, members of Grace Community Church came over to my parents' home to worship, pray, and take communion with our family. I sat on a kitchen barstool beside my sister, overlooking the serene lake view. About the time my dad entered the room (with the help of his best friend and a wheelchair), got positioned in his recliner and greeted everyone, I noticed the most breath-taking rainbow.

The vibrant colors filled the height of the floor-to-ceiling windows and the expanse of one side of the living room to the other. The brilliant shades of beauty overwhelmed me – by far the most magnificent sight I'd ever seen. At that moment, I knew God was about to call my dad home.

Earlier in the day, he hadn't been able to say much except to a few visitors. He'd been out of it the rest of the day, even unable to swallow Tylenol to bring his high fever down. But, somehow now he'd rallied to say a few words and enjoy the fellowship. My dad was even his goofy self and went on for about twenty minutes quoting scripture and talking about how amazing it was that he was able to be with all of us that evening, knowing he'd be with the Lord within twenty-four hours. It was as if he was waiting to see everyone before he could lie down and surrender the fight.

I believe the rainbow was a sign, reminding us of God's promises. And when I saw one the next day outside my parents' bedroom window, as my dad lay unconscious in bed, I knew it was time. This rainbow was further away and more subdued, but it was still just as comforting. I couldn't help but note that it hadn't rained either one of those days.

He took his last breath later that night at 10:10 pm, surrounded by family and friends who held him as he passed. Rainbows will always remind me of my dad. Our family has witnessed quite a few miraculous ones on anniversaries and special occasions throughout the years.

DEATH:
The "Good Fight" is Over

August 17, 2007

Dear family and friends,

"This is the day that the Lord has made; let us rejoice and be glad in it" (Psalm 118:24). Tonight at 10:10 p.m. our dear, sweet Bill was called home to live with our eternal Father. What joy we have in Christ. To God be the Glory now and forever.

Love, Jan

"Precious in the sight of the Lord is the death of his saints."

PSALM 116:15

"O death, where is your victory? O death, where is your sting? The sting of death is sin, and the power of sin is the law. But thanks be to God, who gives us the victory through our Lord Jesus Christ."

1 CORINTHIANS 15:55-57

"Blessed are those who mourn, for they shall be comforted."

MATTHEW 5:4

"For everything there is a season, and a time for every matter under heaven: a time to be born, and a time to die…"

ECCLESIASTES 3:1-2

WIFE'S LETTER:

Jan Williams

Bill and I lived as husband and wife from May 4, 1974, until August 17, 2007. It seems like a lifetime since my beloved husband went to be with the Lord. His life was one of total obedience. I am so humbled to have called him my husband, my friend, and my soul mate.

He loved the Lord with all his soul, mind, and body. He tried to live his life to honor and glorify God even in his illness and death. I am so blessed to have a gracious and merciful Savior that carried me through some of the most difficult days of my life.

Bill had a terminal illness, Multiple Myeloma. We both knew that we would trust God to guide us down the path of medical decisions. We decided that no matter what, we would continue to live each day to the fullest and try to honor God. We truly learned to be thankful for each day and to live each day as nothing more than a day was ever promised to us.

When I think about the progression of Bill's illness at the time of the diagnosis, I realize that God was preparing us for a journey like no other. Over the months of his cancer, Bill's condition was very fragile at times, but he was a fighter. I tried to stay positive and encourage him. It became quite evident that my strength was coming from God. I never felt like I was carrying the burden because our two daughters, son-in-law and granddaughters were standing right beside us. We were so blessed to have been surrounded by our pastors, family, friends, and wonderful doctors and nurses. They prayed for us, drove Bill to doctors' appointments, moved us, and cried with us.

God provided a truly sweet worship time with our family, close friends, pastor, elders, deacons, staff and wives in our home the night before Bill left his earthly home. We sang, "Be Thou My Vision," received Holy Communion, and prayed. God even provided a lovely double rainbow outside our lake view window. When Bill saw it, he said, "God never misses a beat." There had not been any storms or rain in our area, just a visual sign of God's sweet promise of hope.

Bill had a restful night, but he never spoke another word to me. I was able, with the Lord's help, to tell my beloved Bill that I would be okay. I knew that I could never let him go on my own; I got the strength from God. Philippians 4:13 says, "I can do all things through Christ who gives me strength." Bill left us to dwell with our heavenly Father very peacefully and with such dignity. Family and friends surrounded him as he drew his last breath, and the room was completely silent. We all knew that he had fought the good fight as it says in 2 Timothy 4:7-8.

Psalm 118:24 came to me immediately: "This is the day the Lord has made; let us rejoice and be glad in it." That day and time had been ordained by my Sovereign God. His plan is perfect for our lives. I pray that He will continue to guide and direct me in the days ahead. My strength comes only from the Lord, and my joy is in Him.

We had a wonderful love and life together. I miss him so much, beyond words, but I know that he is healed and has gone on ahead to pave the way for other believers.

DAUGHTER'S LETTER:

Melissa Wren Brown

My dad prayed for cancer; he just didn't know it at the time. After reading some of his journal entries and reflecting on conversations with him, it's evident that God does answer our prayers. He answers prayers according to His will, not based on our selfish desires.

 I vividly recall speaking with my dad a year before his diagnosis when he told me he knew he needed to be less involved in his business affairs and more focused on God's work. He said he'd prayed consistently that he'd be taught to number his days so they might be used more productively in God's service and not his own. When my dad prayed for correction and direction, little did he know that cancer would be the answer.

God honored my dad's prayer by giving him what he feared most in the world but what God ordained best for him. He was the healthiest person I've ever known, to the point where he even went through a phase when he added bird seed to his cereal because he thought it might prevent cancer!

God turned my dad's biggest weakness into his most valuable strength. I'm learning through personal experience He does that for all of us if we let Him because He wants to make us more like Christ, and He loves us.

Two years after his death, I got very sick and was diagnosed with several chronic illnesses that have also brought me closer to the love of my life, Jesus Christ. I'm convinced there is no greater delight in this world than falling in love with God.

Reading my dad's emails again has confirmed many of God's promises. I'm thankful for all the challenges I've faced so far because it's made me realize that God really is all that I need. I've never been alone; He's always been there, even when I've pushed Him away.

God's revealed that having a relationship with His Son and enjoying Him, devouring His word, praying for insight, being content, and doing the work He created for us are the things that matter most. It's the purpose to life. (Ephesians 2:10).

I was blessed to receive thirty years with such an awesome earthly father. Thank you gracious Father.

SCRIPTURE REFERENCES - NIV (New International Version)

Psalm 6:5
"No one remembers you when he is dead. Who praises you from the grave?"

Psalm 7:1-2
"O Lord my God, I take refuge in you; save and deliver me from all who pursue me, or they will tear me like a lion and rip me to pieces with no one to rescue me."

Isaiah 55:8
"'For my thoughts are not your thoughts, neither are your ways my ways,' declares the Lord."

1 Corinthians 10:13
"No temptation has seized you except what is common to man. And God is faithful; he will not let you be tempted beyond what you can bear. But when you are tempted, he will also provide a way out so that you can stand up under it."

Job 14:5
"Man's days are determined; you have decreed the number of his months and have set limits he cannot exceed."

Galatians 2:20
"I have been crucified with Christ and I no longer live, but Christ lives in me. The life I live in the body, I live by faith in the Son of God, who loved me and gave himself for me."

Romans 8:28
"And we know that in all things God works for the good of those who love him, who have been called according to his purpose."

Jeremiah 29:11
"For I know the plans I have for you," declares the Lord, "plans to prosper you and not to harm you, plans to give you hope and a future."

Proverbs 19:21
"Many are the plans in a man's heart, but it is the Lord's purpose that prevails."

Job 5:17-18
"Blessed is the man whom God corrects; so do not despise the discipline of the Almighty. For He wounds, but he also binds up; he injures, but His hands also heal."

Acts 14:21-22
"They (Paul and Barnabas) preached the good news in that city and won a large number of disciples. Then they returned to Lystra, Iconium, and Antioch, strengthening the disciples and encouraging them to remain true to the faith. 'We must go through many hardships to enter the kingdom of God,' they said."

Isaiah 48:9-11
"For my own name's sake I delay my wrath; for the sake of my praise I hold it back from you, so as not to cut you off. See, I have refined you, though not as silver, I have tested you in the furnace of affliction. For my own sake, for my own sake, I do this. How can I let myself be defamed? I will not yield my glory to another."

Psalm 115:1
"Not to us, O Lord, not to us but to your name be the glory, because of your love and faithfulness."

Luke 11:3
"Give us each day our daily bread."

Philippians 4:6-7
"Do not be anxious about anything, but in everything, by prayer and petition, with thanksgiving present your request to God. And the peace of God, which transcends all understanding, will guard your hearts and your minds in Christ Jesus."

Proverb 27:17
"As iron sharpens iron, so one man sharpens another."

1 Thessalonians 5:16-18
"Be joyful always; pray continually; give thanks in all circumstances, for this is God's will for you in Christ Jesus."

Habakkuk 3:17-19
"Though the fig tree does not bud and there are no grapes on the vines, though the olive crop fails and the fields produce no food, though there are no sheep in the pen and no cattle in the stalls, yet I will rejoice in the Lord, I will be joyful in God my Savior. The Sovereign Lord is my strength; he makes my feet like the feet of a deer, he enables me to go on the heights."

Acts 17:26
"From one man he made every nation of men, that they should inhabit the whole earth; and he determined the times set for them and the exact places where they should live."

Nahum 1:7
"The Lord is good, a refuge in times of trouble. He cares for those who trust in Him."

Proverbs 21:1
"The king's heart is in the hand of the Lord; he directs it like a watercourse wherever he pleases."

Psalm 4:8
"I will lie down and sleep in peace, for you alone, O Lord, make me dwell in safety."

Matthew 10:29-30
"Are not two sparrows sold for a penny? Yet not one of them will fall to the ground apart from the will of your Father. And even the very hairs of your head are all numbered."

Psalm 55:22
"Cast your cares on the Lord, and He shall sustain you; he will never let the righteous fall."

1 Timothy 4:7-8
"Have nothing to do with godless myths and old wives' tales; rather, train yourself to be godly. For physical training is of some value, but godliness has value for all things, holding promise for both the present life and the life to come."

Isaiah 66:2
"'Has not my hand made all these things, and so they came into being?' declares the Lord. This is the one I esteem: he who is humble and contrite in spirit and trembles at my word."

2 Corinthians 1:3-4
"Praise be to the God and Father of our Lord Jesus Christ, the Father of compassion and the God of all comfort, who comforts us in all our troubles, so that we can comfort those in any trouble with the comfort we ourselves have received from God."

Psalm 30:10-12
"Hear, O Lord, and be merciful to me; O Lord, be my help. You turned my wailing into dancing; you removed my sackcloth and clothed me with joy, that my heart may sing to you and not be silent. O Lord my God, I will give you thanks forever."

Matthew 6:27
"Who of you by worrying can add a single hour to his life?"

Psalm 39:4-5
"Show me, O Lord, my life's end and the number of days; let me know how fleeting is my life. You have made my days a mere handbreadth; the span of my years is as nothing before you. Each man's life is but a breath."

Proverbs 17:27-28
"A man of knowledge uses words with restraint, and a man of understanding is even-tempered. Even a fool is thought wise if he keeps silent, and discerning if he holds his tongue."

Hebrews 12:2
"Let us fix our eyes on Jesus, the author and perfecter of our faith, who for the joy set before him endured the

cross, scorning its shame, and sat down at the right hand of the throne of God."

James 1:2-4
"Consider it pure joy, my brothers, whenever you face trials of many kinds, because you know that the testing of your faith develops perseverance. Perseverance must finish its work so that you may be mature and complete, not lacking anything."

Psalm 139:14-16
"I praise you because I am fearfully and wonderfully made; your works are wonderful, I know that full well. My frame was not hidden from you when I was made in the secret place. When I was woven together in the depths of the earth, your eyes saw my unformed body. All the days ordained for me were written in your book before one of them came to be."

John 6:37 "All that the Father gives me will come to me, and whoever comes to me I will never drive away."

John 10:27
"My sheep listen to my voice; I know them, and they follow me. I give them eternal life, and they shall never perish; no one can snatch them out of my hand."

Matthew 6:34
"Therefore, do not worry about tomorrow, for tomorrow will worry about itself. Each day has enough trouble of its own."

1 Peter 1:6-7
"In this you greatly rejoice, though now for a little while you may have had to suffer grief in all kinds of trials. These have come so that your faith – of greater worth than gold, which perishes even though refined by fire – may be proved genuine and may result in praise, glory and honor when Jesus Christ is revealed."

Judges 7:2
"The Lord said to Gideon, 'You have too many men for me to deliver Midian into their hands. In order that Israel may not boast against me that her own strength has saved her, announce now to the people, 'Anyone who trembles with fear may turn back and leave Mount Gilead.' So twenty-two thousand men left, while ten thousand remained."

Psalm 31:3
"Since you are my rock and my fortress, for the sake of your name lead and guide me."

Additional Scripture

The following scriptures were some used during Bill's "Celebration of Life" ceremony - taken from his most recent memory verse pack that he was known for carrying. Bill was a Christian the last 20 years of his life and spent those years loving and getting to know the Lord more intimately by hiding portions of the Holy Bible in his heart. He knew over a thousand verses by memory.

2 Timothy 4:7
"I have fought the good fight, I have finished the race, I have kept the faith."

Psalm 13:6
"I will sing to the Lord, for he has been good to me."

Romans 5:3-4
"Not only so, but we also rejoice in our sufferings, because we know that suffering produces perseverance; perseverance, character; and character, hope."

Isaiah 43:1b
"Fear not, for I have redeemed you; I have summoned you by name; you are mine."

Psalm 105:4
"Look to the Lord and his strength; seek his face always."

Psalm 118:5-6
"In my anguish I cried out to the Lord, and he answered by setting me free. The Lord is with me; I will not be afraid. What can man do to me?"

John 14:27
"Peace I leave with you; my peace I give you. I do not give to you as the world gives. Do not let your hearts be troubled and do not be afraid."

Other Scripture

Romans 8:18
"For I consider that the sufferings of this present time are not worth comparing with the glory that is to be revealed to us."

2 Corinthians 4:16
"So we do not give up. Our physical body is becoming older and weaker, but our spirit inside us is made new every day."

2 Corinthians 4:8
"We have troubles all around us, but we are not defeated. We do not know what to do, but we do not give up the hope of living."

Bill's Biography

Clyde (Bill) Williams Jr, 56, of Granbury, Texas was born August 30, 1950 – August 17, 2007, in Clovis, New Mexico. His parents, Clyde and Nona Williams also of Granbury, reared him in Roaring Springs, Texas.

Bill became a Christian at the age of 36 and spent the last 20 years of his life loving and serving his Lord and Savior Jesus Christ with all his heart and sharing this with those around him. He was a member and elder at Grace Community Church in Glen Rose, TX.

He graduated from high school in Comanche, Texas, played basketball at Texas Weslyan and graduated from the University of Texas. Bill married his sweetheart, Janet Gallagher, of Corpus Christi, Texas in Austin on May 4, 1974.

He bought into his father's grocery business and together, they successfully grew a small chain of 16 Thrift Mart Food Stores, to serve much of central Texas for 22 years. In 1995, Bill retired from the grocery business and continued managing his real estate portfolio.

Over the years he was privileged to serve on several boards including: Hannah House, Habitat for Humanity, Heritage National Bank, Coca Cola, Affiliated Foods, and Thomas Bros. Grass.

He is survived by his wife, Jan, after 33 years of marriage; daughters, Melissa Brown and her husband, Robert; two grandchildren Daniel and Micah; Kendra Fox and her husband Kevin; three granddaughters Marley, Tessa and Harper, who all live in Granbury; as well as his sisters, Cye Gossett; Karen Davis, and brothers Jamey, Kerry, and Jerry Williams, and other family and friends too numerous to count.

Info

Grace Community Church of Glen Rose, Texas
2008 Hwy 56 North
PO Box 2186
Glen Rose, TX 76043
254-897-3320
www.gccministries.org

StoneWater Church
911 E. Hwy 377 Texana Plaza
Granbury, TX 76048
817-579-9175
www.StoneWaterChurch.com

Resources

Multiple Myeloma Cancer

Definition from the **Mayo Clinic**

"Multiple myeloma is a cancer of your plasma cells, a type of white blood cells present in your bone marrow. Plasma cells normally make proteins called antibodies to help you fight infections. In multiple myeloma, a group of abnormal plasma cells (myeloma cells) multiplies, raising the number of plasma cells to a higher than normal level. Since these cells normally make proteins, the level of abnormal proteins in your blood also may go up. Health problems caused by multiple myeloma can affect your bones, immune system, kidneys and red blood cell count."

International Myeloma Foundation
Non-profit organization featuring research, clinical trials, events, and fundraising.
www.myeloma.org

Cancer - general
www.cancer.gov

Multiple Myeloma Survivor Stories
This site has treatment histories written by patients
http://mm.acor.org/

Suggested Readings

1. "Heaven" by Randy Alcorn (the last book Bill read before he died)
2. "90 Minutes in Heaven" by Don Piper (one of the last books Bill read)
3. "The Attributes of God" by Arthur W. Pink
4. "Don't Waste Your Life" by John Piper
5. "The Pursuit of God" by A.W. Tozer
6. "The Sovereignty of God" by A.W. Pink
7. "The Holiness of God" by R.C. Sproul
8. "The Christian's Secret of a Happy Life" by Hannah Whitall Smith
9. "Sinners in the Hands of an Angry God" by Jonathan Edwards
10. "A Grief Observed" by C.S. Lewis

The purpose of this book is to encourage those who are suffering and provide a Biblical perspective on how to glorify God during trials. Thank you for taking the time to read this true story and passing it on to those in need.

This compilation is a passion project created to spread the hope God gives each one of us during our trials if we believe in His Son, Jesus Christ.

Free copies are available to those who aren't able to contribute.

Donations are accepted to cover the cost of printing and giving to charity.

For more information on how to order books at cost and in bulk for your church, hospital or other facility, please contact:

**Melissa Wren Brown at
melwrenbrown@gmail.com
Books are also available on www.amazon.com.
Also see: http://melissawren.blogspot.com**

Made in the USA
Charleston, SC
11 January 2013